I0804331

IMAGES
of America

CAPE HATTERAS LIGHTHOUSE

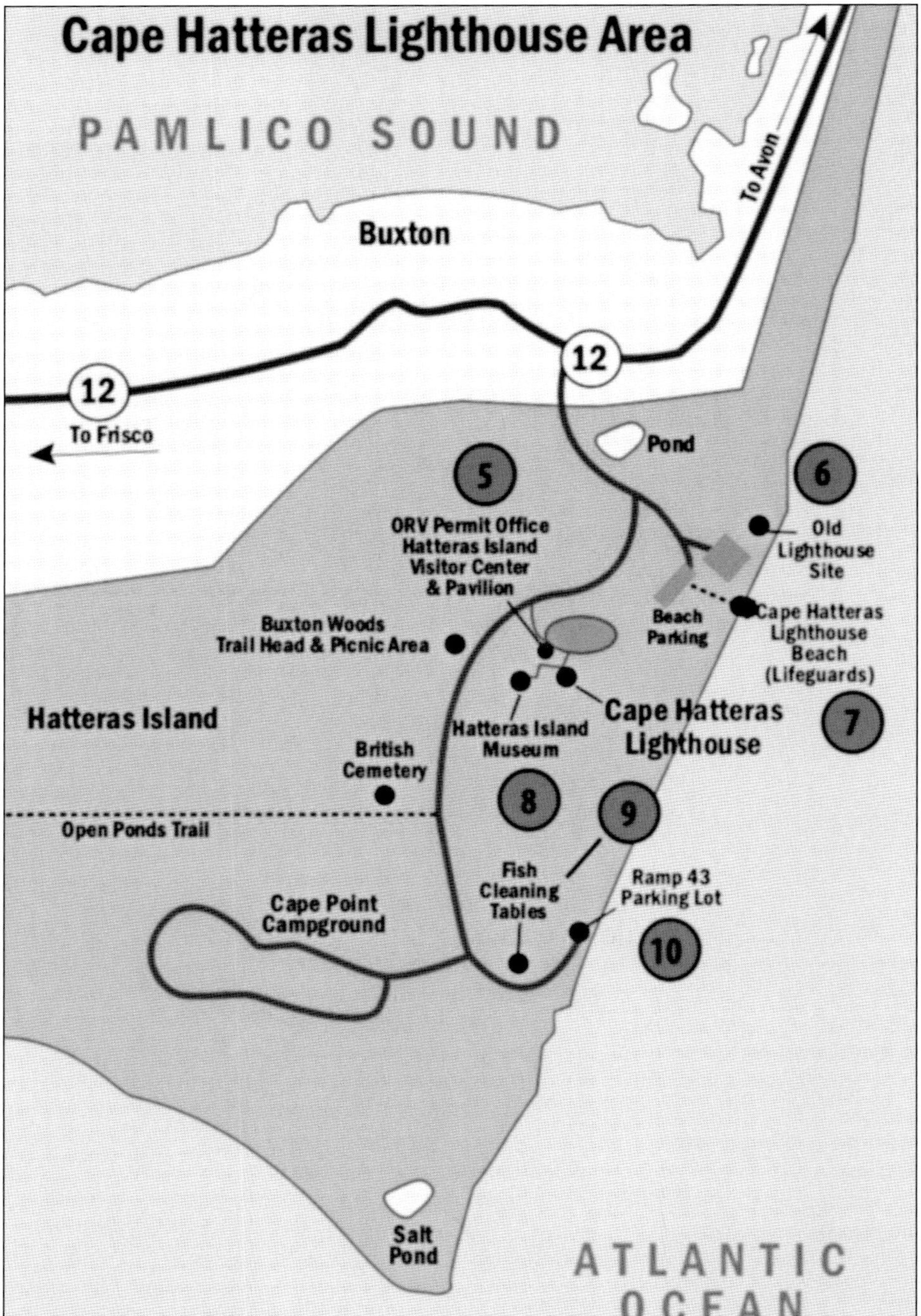

This map shows the Cape Hatteras National Seashore Lighthouse area near Buxton, North Carolina. (Courtesy of the National Park Service.)

On the Cover: Pictured on the cover is local Mary Ormond White Fuller walking the beach with the Cape Hatteras Lighthouse in the background. (Photograph by Bill Gulley; courtesy of the North Carolina Collection Photographic Archives, the Wilson Library, University of North Carolina at Chapel Hill.)

IMAGES
of America

CAPE HATTERAS LIGHTHOUSE

Mary Ellen Riddle and Douglas Stover

ARCADIA
PUBLISHING

ISBN 978-1-4671-0613-9

Published by Arcadia Publishing
Charleston, South Carolina

Printed in the United States of America

Library of Congress Control Number: 2020945344

For all general information, please contact Arcadia Publishing:
Telephone 843-853-2070
Fax 843-853-0044
E-mail sales@arcadiapublishing.com
For customer service and orders:
Toll-Free 1-888-313-2665

Visit us on the Internet at www.arcadiapublishing.com

This book is dedicated to the lighthouse keepers, assistants, employees, and their families and to August Lee Riddle, a new light in the world.

Contents

Acknowledgments

Special thanks to John Havel, whose dedication and contributions truly made this book possible. Thanks also to Kevin Duffus for his keen proofreader's eye. Dave Greider's love for the Cape Hatteras Lighthouse helped inspire this project, and, of course, Jami Lanier at the National Park Service (NPS) aided us in procuring information and photographs. Gratitude goes to our editor Caroline Anderson, who helped us achieve our deadlines and final goal at every twist and turn.

Unless otherwise noted, all photographs are courtesy of the National Park Service, Outer Banks Group.

Introduction

Flashing bright against night skies, lighthouses captivate the imaginations of humankind. Towering above a flat landscape with an expansive view of the Carolina heavens, the Cape Hatteras Lighthouse is one of the most famous of these sentinels. Its connection to the sea creates a magnetic attraction, and like a great novel, it brings atmosphere, mystery, and adventure to its pages. This is a tale of famous and ordinary, of big and small, and of life and death propelled by a cast of characters bound to nature.

Lighthouses were erected for navigators as daymarks and to warn sailors of dangerous coastal conditions. Cape Hatteras was infamous for shoals and storms, and with a global trade route located off its shore, heavy traffic made a daymark essential. Explorers, naval commanders, and freight captains traveling the Gulf Stream had to navigate around the infamous Diamond Shoals at the tip of the cape—many vessels grounding hopelessly on the shallow sandbars. Over the years, more than 2,000 ships wrecked in the waters off the Outer Banks, for it was an essential route for national and global interests.

Transport vessels riding the Gulf Stream past Cape Hatteras were carrying the necessities of life, including fuel, lumber, and food. With its flashing pattern guiding mariners through darkened and dangerous seascapes and its spiral black-and-white stripes illustrating location, the Cape Hatteras Lighthouse was not only vital for sailors and the economy, but it also illustrated humankind's ability to adapt to or overcome natural challenges through innovation, blood, sweat, and tears.

Tempered by perseverance and teamwork, the Cape Hatteras Lighthouse endured foul weather, erosion, war, vandalism, neglect, and relocation. Regardless of the trials, stationing a light at Cape Hatteras was a worthy endeavor. One sentinel (1803) and an heightened version of it (1854) stood guard at Cape Hatteras before the infamous black-and-white 1870s lighthouse was built to the necessary standards. As with an oceanfront house needing upkeep, repairs have been continual since the first lighthouse was erected.

Presenting an abbreviated chronology of the management and technological advancements of the lighthouse system is necessary to understand the number of steps that went into helping make the country's coasts and waterways safe and to bringing a lighthouse to Cape Hatteras. As they say, no man is an island. And no lighthouse would exist without collaboration. But it is important to note that time, inexperience, and political wrangling prevented the Cape Hatteras Lighthouse from immediately meeting the needs of mariners.

Before 1789, the original 13 colonies were responsible for providing the necessary navigational aids. Lighthouses were built near large trade ports. But the sentinels on the Atlantic Coast were absent.

In April 1789, the US House of Representatives began to discuss the possibility of a lighthouses bill. On August 7, 1789, Pres. George Washington signed an Act for the Establishment and Support of Light-Houses, Beacons, Buoys, and Public Piers. This gave the government jurisdiction over all preexisting navigational aids in the country. A budget was included for the payment of keepers and maintenance. The Department of the Treasury oversaw the newly formed United

States Lighthouse Establishment (USLHE). The USLHE became responsible for 12 operational lighthouses and four in the process of being built.

In the beginning, treasury secretary Alexander Hamilton managed the lighthouses. In 1792, responsibility was assigned to the commissioner of revenue, Tench Coxe.

Hamilton understood firsthand the danger of traversing the Atlantic Ocean. He was traveling from St. Croix to Boston in the late 1770s when a mishap occurred. The vessel he was on caught fire and flooded. The location of the occurrence is unknown, but the incident could have influenced his interest in safe navigation.

On February 20, 1794, Hamilton submitted the *Report Relative to a Lighthouse on Cape Hatteras* to the president of the US Senate. Within three months, Pres. George Washington approved purchasing land to build a "first rate" lighthouse and supplied everything that was needed to do so, including supplies and salaries. A local family sold land for the project, and a builder was chosen to construct the first 90-foot Cape Hatteras Lighthouse.

In 1812, the patent for a new lantern with reflecting and magnifying qualities was purchased for $20,000 from a former ship captain, Winslow Lewis. Reflecting design elements of the Swiss Argand–style lamp and parabolic reflector, the lantern also used glass with a green tinge at the front of the lamp. This negatively affected the range of the light. Yet all the lighthouses were operating with Lewis's lanterns by 1815. It took the government 25 years to remove all the green lenses.

On August 1, 1820, a memorable figure became responsible for navigational aids. Operating under the Department of the Treasury (after responsibility had moved back and forth between the secretary of treasury and the Department of Commerce), the fifth auditor, Stephen Pleasonton, was appointed the general superintendent of lights. Collectors of customs at the individual ports became the superintendents of lights. They were fully responsible for all aspects concerning the lighthouses, from issues with personnel and building to yearly visits to the lighthouse sites. All important decisions were made by the general superintendent, such as merging multiple supplies contracts into one. Such a contract was awarded to Winslow Lewis at $35.87 per lamp per year. Stephen Pleasonton believed in Lewis due to his abilities and nautical experience.

It has been stated that because of this relationship, there was scant technological growth under the general superintendent's rule. This included his rejection of the idea to have Fresnel lenses installed despite their having achieved technological success by 1822. Thwarting progress could have been Winslow Lewis's monetary stake with his patented lenses and the $5,000 cost for a first-order Fresnel lens.

In time, American mariners began comparing domestic lighthouses to those in Europe. Multiple complaints arose about poor construction, use of funds, inadequate lamps, and mismanagement of the USLHE.

As a result, the Board of Navy Commissioners was tasked with doing a study that determined that 31 of the new lighthouses proposed by Congress were not necessary and that the USLHE was successful but that a new office, the Auditor of the Department of State and General Superintendent of the Lighthouse Establishment, should replace Pleasonton's position. Yet Pleasonton continued in his role.

On June 7, 1838, Congress sectioned the Atlantic Coast into six districts. The current superintendents were replaced with naval officers. While their reports on the lighthouses differed to some extent, the majority noted the poor quality of light. Congress called for a test to be conducted comparing the Fresnel lenses being used in Europe to America's reflector lamps. A first-order fixed Fresnel lens and a second-order revolving lens were purchased behind Pleasonton's back. In 1840, they were put into place and tested in the towers that looked over New York Harbor. The test was successful. Pleasonton was not swayed, though, and stayed steadfast in his position.

Dissatisfaction continued. Attempts were made to better regulate the USLHE, and studies were pursued. It was not until 1847 that the responsibility for the light stations moved from the fifth auditor to the Corps of Topographical Engineers. "On March 3, 1851, Congress approved An Act Making Appropriations for Light House, Light Boats, Buoys, &c," according to the *Cape Hatteras Historic Structure Report*. The United States Lighthouse Board (USLHB) was eventually created as part of that act. The board was tasked with examining all aspects of the lighthouse operation. A lengthy report was submitted, including recommendation that Fresnel lenses be installed in every lighthouse.

The USLHB divided the country into 12 lighthouse districts. The Cape Hatteras Lighthouse fell into the fifth district, which covered Metomkin Inlet, Virginia, south to New River, North Carolina. Eventually both a military officer—working as the inspector and general superintendent—and an engineer were appointed to every district.

By 1854, the focal plane of the original Cape Hatteras Lighthouse was elevated to 150 feet.

The establishment of the USLHB resulted in the lighthouse rising to the top of the list to receive a Fresnel lens. An Augustin Henry Lepaute lens was ordered from France, and it was installed in the 1854 red and white Cape Hatteras Lighthouse.

On April 12, 1861, the Civil War commenced. Pres. Abraham Lincoln called for a blockade of the southern coast to impede the Confederacy from bringing in supplies for war and revenue sources. By April 24, the Confederacy had darkened all the lighthouses, and the Cape Hatteras Lighthouse lamp was extinguished. The Confederate States Lighthouse Bureau (CSLB) was created and divided the Confederacy into four lighthouse districts, but navigational aids suffered during the war. The 1854 Cape Hatteras Lighthouse lens and others were removed and hidden, lightships were sunk, and management was disrupted due to the call to military duty.

Much needed to be rectified after the war to reestablish the country's lighthouses. In 1870, a new Cape Hatteras Lighthouse was built. Multiple changes in management occurred over the years, and the number of lighthouse districts grew. In 1910, the United States Light House Service was formed under the Department of Commerce, according to the *Cape Hatteras Structure Report*. It is important to note that between 1852 and 1910, lighthouse aids expanded by more than 3,000. A commissioner of lighthouses was hired, and additional districts were added, managed by a district inspector. Every district also included an engineer, an assistant, and a clerk.

With World War I on the horizon, the United States Light House Service was transferred to the Department of War and the Navy. The tenders and personnel at the light stations were tasked with reporting sightings of submarines and vessels on the surface. The waters off Cape Hatteras saw action. In early August 1918, U-140 destroyed Diamond Shoals lightship LV-71 and the freighter SS *Merak*. By mid-August, U-117 set her sights on and sank the British steamship *Mirlo*.

By 1933, the lamp was electrified. The clockwork mechanism and weight system still turned the lens. This changed in 1934 when the mechanism was also electrified.

The number of navigational aids more than doubled, and employees were let go due to advancements such as utilizing automatic navigational aids as well as the other improvements.

In 1939, the Presidential Reorganization Act transferred the Bureau of Lighthouses from the Department of Commerce to the United States Coast Guard, under the Department of the Treasury.

This year marked the last one the final Cape Hatteras principal keeper, Unaka B. Jennette, held his post.

In January 1942, the Coast Guard leased the lighthouse as a watchtower to scan for U-boats that were patrolling shipping lanes. During World War II, the waters off the Outer Banks, dubbed "Torpedo Junction" due to U-boat action, saw a loss of 86 Allied vessels and four U-boats. Under the glow of the Cape Hatteras Lighthouse, explosions rattled island windows, emblazoned night skies, and covered beaches with oil.

Over time, changes to the beacon continued. In the 1960s, the thrust was on automation of the light stations, and by the 1970s, only one civilian keeper remained. Following 1989, the days of manning the stations were over.

In the 1990s, the historic move of the Cape Hatteras Lighthouse became a necessity due to erosion caused by encroachment of the sea, the unruly wonder it was meant to guard. The standoff resulted in relocation and was called the move of the century. Today, the lighthouse continues to light the way. There really is no end to a lighthouse story, for as long as there are mariners, there always will be a need for a light to guide their way.

Cape Hatteras Lighthouse will focus on the historic highlights, its people and technology, and the future of this iconic structure. Vintage photographs lend insight into a centuries-long story that began when the first mariners passed a darkened Cape Hatteras, perhaps running aground on its shoals or losing their way with no daymark to guide them.

December 2020 marked the 150th anniversary of lighting the 1870 Cape Hatteras Lighthouse. The storied sentinel encourages us to embrace both the historic and humble—the role global collaboration played in the construction of a coastal light as well as quiet acts such as a keeper climbing 269 stairs daily to light a lifesaving lamp.

One

From Darkness into Light

For centuries, sailors traveled the Gulf Stream to gain time in their journey. The swift force brought many ships past Cape Hatteras. Shoals and weather hindered journeys and caused shipwrecks, resulting in the area's moniker "Graveyard of the Atlantic." Being without a lighthouse off the cape hindered American shipping. In the late 1700s, Congress authorized construction of the first Cape Hatteras Lighthouse, seen here. (Redrawn by John Havel; courtesy of John Havel.)

On February 20, 1794, Secretary of the Treasury Alexander Hamilton, pictured here, sent a report to the Senate regarding building a lighthouse at Cape Hatteras. Congress awarded the funds. Pres. George Washington approved an act to cede the needed land to the United States; furnish a contract for construction, supplies, and wages for building supervision; and stipulate that the lights be distinctive from one another to prevent navigational errors. (Courtesy of the Library of Congress.)

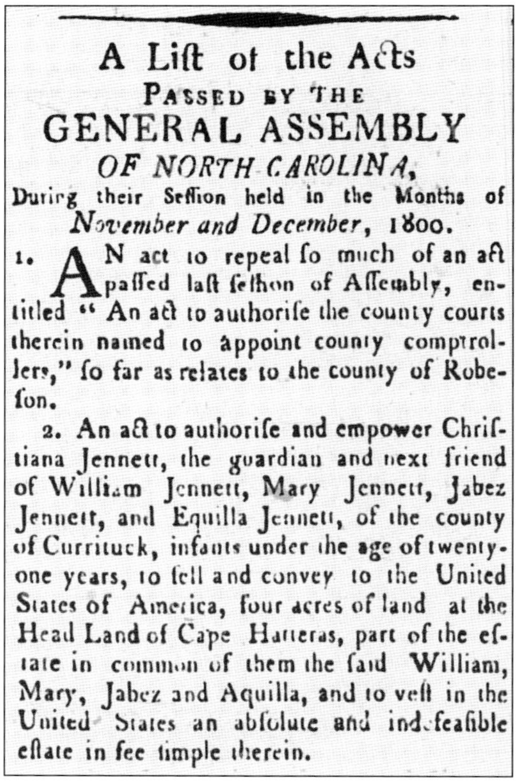

A Liſt of the Acts
PASSED BY THE
GENERAL ASSEMBLY
OF NORTH CAROLINA,
During their Seſſion held in the Months of
November and December, 1800.

1. AN act to repeal ſo much of an act paſſed laſt ſeſſion of Aſſembly, entitled "An act to authoriſe the county courts therein named to appoint county comptrollers," ſo far as relates to the county of Robeſon.

2. An act to authoriſe and empower Chriſtiana Jennett, the guardian and next friend of William Jennett, Mary Jennett, Jabez Jennett, and Equilla Jennett, of the county of Currituck, infants under the age of twenty-one years, to ſell and convey to the United States of America, four acres of land at the Head Land of Cape Hatteras, part of the eſtate in common of them the ſaid William, Mary, Jabez and Aquilla, and to veſt in the United States an abſolute and indefeaſible eſtate in fee ſimple therein.

As seen in this period newspaper clipping, four acres of land were purchased for the Cape Hatteras Light Station for $50 from five members of the Jennett family. The Currituck County Registrar's Office notes that the sale was registered on February 25, 1801. It is interesting to note that a descendant of the Jennetts was the last of a long line of keepers at the Cape Hatteras Lighthouse. (Courtesy of the *Wilmington Gazette*, January 1, 1801, newspapers.com.)

Money was appropriated between the years 1797 and 1803 for the erection of the lighthouse. Locals displayed no interest in taking on the building project, so advertisements were posted in government offices from "Maine to North Carolina," according to the *Cape Hatteras Historic Structure Report*. An initiative was suggested to place advertisements in newspapers in six states. While bids came in, none of them met with approval. Eventually, former Massachusetts congressperson Henry Dearborn, pictured here, stepped up to the plate. (Courtesy of the Library of Congress.)

Henry Dearborn's bid was reviewed and found wanting due to lack of necessary construction, material, and transportation details. He went back to the drawing board and then resubmitted a proposal in the fall of 1798, which Pres. John Adams (pictured here) approved. On October 31, 1978, the contract was signed by Dearborn, and on February 14, 1799, the government added its John Hancock to the document. (Courtesy of the Library of Congress.)

Henry Dearborn was also building a lighthouse at Shell Castle Island. By October, the work at both sites was moving forward. Dearborn returned to Hatteras in March 1800, and work began on the foundation. The workers put in the first course of stone for the base. Come July, the tower was 12 feet above grade, and the second-floor framing was finished. At month's end, a number of crew members fell ill with one dying. Henry Dearborn left the site, putting Dudley B. Hobart in charge. Within a few months, Hobart instructed the rest of the men to return home. They had finished the Cape Hatteras keepers' quarters. In 1801, Pres. Thomas Jefferson appointed Dearborn secretary of war. Then, with some fits and starts due to illness, the project progressed, and building resumed in the spring of 1802. Workers finished the masonry work in June, and it was time to procure lanterns. In August 1802, the lighthouse was complete except for its lighting. Pres. Thomas Jefferson named Adam Gaskin as the first keeper, and Gaskin began work on December 29, 1802, being paid $333 per year. Seen here are the remains of the 1803 lighthouse foundation.

Over the years, lighthouse repairs and replacements occurred due to inefficiency, weather damage, wear, and fire. In 1803, the oil cisterns were replaced with larger ones that housed 2,000 gallons. In September 1806, the lantern sustained damage in a storm, and the lamp went dark. It took more than a month to complete the repairs. Eventually, the lighting apparatus was replaced. Around 1815, the federal government contracted Winslow Lewis of Boston to bring the nation's lighthouses up to date. At Cape Hatteras, he installed 18 Argand-style lamps (an example is pictured here) and parabolic reflectors on a chandelier in the lantern, which "rotated via a clockwork mechanism," according to the *Cape Hatteras Historic Structure Report*. Despite the improvements, complaints arose in the spring of 1817 and were blamed on the deficient quality of the oil. Complaints came again in late 1819, and dirty reflectors and lamp chimneys were discovered. The following year, Stephen Pleasonton, the fifth auditor of the Treasury Department, was put in charge of supervising the country's lighthouses. Complaints about Cape Hatteras lighthouse came to his attention, including the one below published in the *National Gazette* on March 13, 1821, written by ship commanders and merchants. (Right, courtesy of the Library of Congress; below, courtesy of the *National Gazette*, March 13, 1821, newspapers.com.)

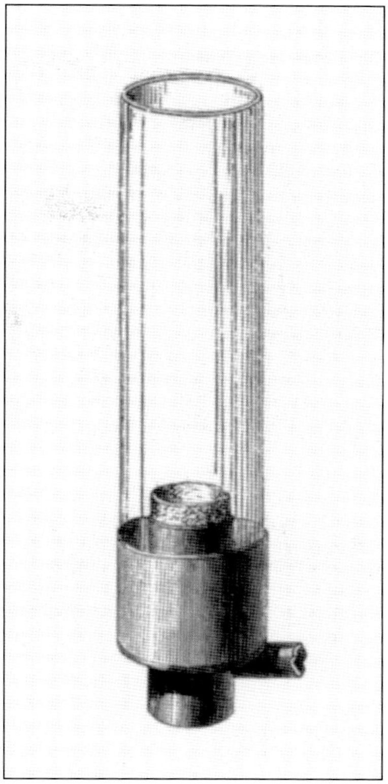

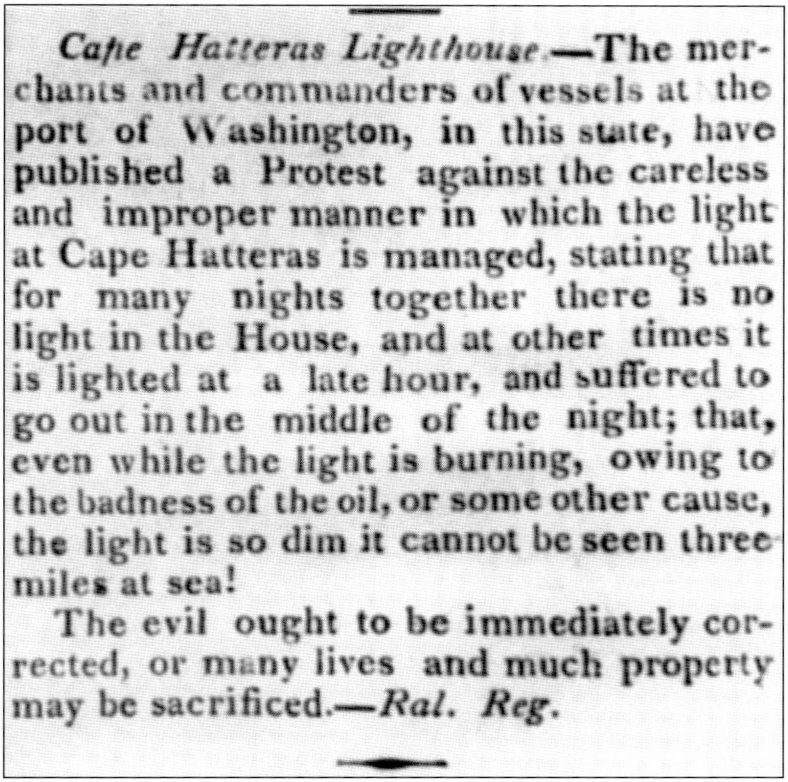

Cape Hatteras Lighthouse.—The merchants and commanders of vessels at the port of Washington, in this state, have published a Protest against the careless and improper manner in which the light at Cape Hatteras is managed, stating that for many nights together there is no light in the House, and at other times it is lighted at a late hour, and suffered to go out in the middle of the night; that, even while the light is burning, owing to the badness of the oil, or some other cause, the light is so dim it cannot be seen three miles at sea!

The evil ought to be immediately corrected, or many lives and much property may be sacrificed.—*Ral. Reg.*

As a result, in April 1821, Pleasonton, pictured here, let keeper Joseph Farrow go and appointed Pharoah Farrow as the new keeper. A recommendation to backfill the foundation with sand was fulfilled. In time, the keepers' quarters needed replacement due to disrepair. On July 21, 1828, Pharoah Farrow sold 40 acres for $200. The land was for the new keepers' housing and, in time, for the 1870 lighthouse. In 1830, Farrow lost his job due to living away from the light station while relegating his duties to several of his enslaved people. Isaac Farrow took his place. Within six years, the lighthouse needed a new lantern. Winslow Lewis received a contract to build an 18-lamp lantern, but in 1840, the lamps, once again, needed changing. Over time, a new lantern with fifteen 21-inch reflectors was installed. In 1850, Pleasonton decided it was important to enclose the lighthouse with a board fence and filled the inner space with brush to hopefully protect the foundation from the elements. Brush filler, seen below, was also used at a later time. (Left, courtesy of the US State Department.)

"In 1847, Congress removed the responsibility for the construction of new light stations from the fifth auditor, Stephen Pleasonton, and transferred it to the Corps of Topographical Engineers," according to the *Cape Hatteras Lighthouse Historic Structure Report*. (Pleasonton eventually left his appointment overseeing the United State Lighthouse Establishment in 1852.) In 1850, complaints arose about an absentee keeper, the cleanliness of the lantern, and other challenges, including fog attributed to the lighthouse being too tall. A study by Benjamin Isherwood, chief engineer in the US Navy, seen here, reported that "the station had nearly new reflectors with clean lamps, the keeper was reputable, the light was sufficient, and that the prevalent fog was indeed a severe problem." He regarded the fog challenge as humankind's inability to overcome nature. The following year, Lt. David D. Porter, US Navy, wrote: "Hatteras Light, the most important on our coast, and, without doubt, the worst light in the world." The Gulf Stream brought sailors close to the shoals, and the inadequate light gave no confidence, he explained. Porter suggested that Hatteras have a revolving light of great intensity and be raised an added 15 feet. (Courtesy of the Library of Congress.)

Naval officers agreed that the light was woefully insufficient. The captain of the steamship *Ludlow* said the Cape Hatteras lighthouse "should be one of the most powerful . . . as it is a point which coasters wish to turn close, south bound, to avoid the Gulf Stream." The sailors were fearful of grounding on the shoals. In early March 1851, Congress passed the act regarding appropriations for "Light House, Light Boats, Buoys, &c." It called for the secretary of the treasury to form the United States Lighthouse Board, and Commodore William B. Shubrick, at left, was named president of that board. The United States Lighthouse Board reported of the Cape Hatteras light: "There is perhaps no Light on the entire coast of the United States of greater value to the commerce and navigation of the country than this. There is no single light on the coast believed to require renovation more than this does. An elevation of one-hundred-and-fifty-feet, and a first-class illuminating apparatus, are imperiously demanded, and without unnecessary delay." This comparison table shows brightness and focal length. (Left, courtesy of the Library of Congress.)

COMPARATIVE TABLE OF LENS ORDERS

Original Fresnel Orders: Order		Nº of Lamp Wicks	Oil Consumption per Hour: gm.	oz.	Relative Brightness (6th Order = 1)	Modern Lens Orders (U.S.A.)	Focal Length: mm.	in.	Lower Reflector: mm.	in.	Central Refractor: mm.	in.	Upper Reflector: mm.	in.	Total: mm	in.	Approximate Weight of Assembled Lens: kg.	lbs.	Use
1ST		4	750	26.25	17.69	1ST	920	36.22	539	21.22	980	38.58	1001	39.40	2590	101.97	5800	12,800	LARGEST SEACOAST LIGHTS
2ND		3	500	17.5	11.54	2ND	750	27.55	378	14.88	854	33.62	810	31.89	2069	81.46	1600	3,530	GREAT LAKES LIGHTHOUSES, SEACOASTS ISLANDS, SOUNDS
3RD	LARGE	2	200	7	3.85	3RD	500	19.69	278	10.94	660	25.98	593	23.35	1576	62.05	900	1,985	SEACOAST, SOUNDS RIVER ENTRY, BAYS, CHANNELS, RANGE LIGHTS
	SMALL	1	150	5.25	2.31	4TH	250	9.84	144	5.67	300	11.81	358	14.09	722	28.43	200 TO 300	440 TO 660	SHOALS, REEFS, HARBOR LIGHTS, ISLANDS IN RIVERS AND HARBORS
4TH	LARGE	2	90	3.15	1.23	5TH	182.5	7.19	105	4.13	226	8.90	196	7.72	541	21.30	120 TO 200	265 TO 440	BREAKWATERS RIVER LIGHTS CHANNEL, SMALL ISLANDS IN SOUNDS.
	SMALL	1	90	3.15	1	6TH	150	5.9	84	3.31	180	7.09	157	6.18	433	17.05	100	220	PIER OR BREAKWATER LIGHTS IN HARBORS.

The United States Lighthouse Board went into action and positioned a buoy on Diamond Shoals and off Cape Hatteras. An engineer was tasked with figuring out how high they could raise the lighthouse and what was needed to place a first-order Fresnel lens and lantern. In time, lightships such as LV-71, were used at Diamond Shoals. Meanwhile, an unfinished lens manufactured by the Henry-LePaute Company for Sand Key Lighthouse in Florida was finished for Cape Hatteras. The 1854 brick tower was heightened by approximately 35 feet, seen above. Added atop the brick addition was an eight-foot-tall, cast-iron watch room and 15-foot-high lantern and dome. The focal plane of the first-order lens was 140 feet above the lighthouse base. The revolving Fresnel lens could be seen for 20 miles. The lower part of the lighthouse (70 feet) was painted white with the upper part painted red, allowing the sentinel to stand out rather than blend into the environment. (Courtesy of the Cape Hatteras Light Station, RG 26, National Archives and Records Administration.)

In 1853, prior to installation, the new lens appeared at the Exhibition of the Industry of All Nations in New York City's Crystal Palace, as seen here. US topographical engineer George Gordon Meade went to New York to put together the new first-order lens at the show, which was the second first-order lens in the United States. Meade gave this report in Philadelphia's *American and Gazette*: "Fancy a twenty-four sided structure of glass . . . the whole being about ten feet high and six feet in diameter . . . being composed of . . . prisms so scientifically calculated, so artistically constructed, and so nicely put together, that each prism refracts the ray from one of its surfaces, reflects it from the second, and refracting it again from the third, shoots it forth in a sun like beam of light." The installation of the Fresnel lens at the Cape Hatteras Lighthouse by keeper William O'Neal and a lampist occurred sometime after March 1854. (Courtesy of the New York Public Library Digital Collections.)

Two

Guarding Liberty and Light

The dawning of the Civil War played a role in the history of the lighthouse. Shortly after his election on March 4, 1861, and the Union loss of the Battle of Fort Sumter, Pres. Abraham Lincoln, pictured here, called for a blockade of the southern coast to stop the South from getting needed supplies and revenue. As a result, by April 24, all the lighthouses in Confederate states were extinguished. (Courtesy of the Library of Congress.)

The Confederacy situated Fort Hatteras and Fort Clark at Hatteras Inlet to protect the Cape Hatteras Lighthouse. Due to significant grounding of Union vessels, it was deemed necessary to light the sentinel. In August 1861, seven warships were sent to the area. The Union bombarded the forts and were victorious. Shown above is the attack on the forts. It marked the first Union-won battle in the Civil War, the first amphibious assault, and the first joint Army/Navy venture in the war. (Courtesy of the Library of Congress.)

It was discovered that the Cape Hatteras Fresnel lens had disappeared, and an expedition left to search for it. Word was it had been transported upriver. Comdr. S.C. Rowan, pictured at right, made threats to track down the guilty parties and "take all the property I can find that will reimburse the Government" and "frighten the people out of their boots unless the lens is returned." The lens was unguarded in a warehouse in Washington, North Carolina, as lighthouse superintendent H.F. Hancock had fled. The warehouse owner, John Meyers, took the boxes filled with the lens parts by way of the riverboat *Governor Morehead* to Tarboro. The cargo was given to an Army quartermaster, Capt. George H. Brown. An agent arrived for the pickup of the lens but disappeared with the funding. Dr. David Tayloe of Washington, North Carolina, seen below, agreed to help if given a boxcar. "On April 14, Tayloe rolled out of Tarboro, accompanied by forty-four boxes, two cases, sixty-four castings, fourteen fixtures, and two sheets of copper," according to the *Cape Hatteras Lighthouse Historic Structure Report*. He arrived at his family's Hibernia Plantation where he hid the lens in a country storehouse. (Right, courtesy of the Library of Congress; below, courtesy of Lisa Cooper.)

A new lens was needed for the lighthouse as the steamer lamp being used was insufficient. Meanwhile, the Confederate army tried to recapture the island. At sunrise, half a dozen Confederate steamships landed at the northern end of the island at Chicamacomico. Stationed there were 600 Union soldiers. The soldiers ran farther than 23 miles from the ships. Seen above is an illustration of the conflict. (Courtesy of the Library of Congress.)

Unfortunately for the Confederates, they grounded on a sandbar and were unable to cut off the fleeing soldiers. The Union troops arrived at the lighthouse around midnight. They were backed by the Ninth New York Regiment. In an about face, the Union chased their enemy back to where the Confederate ships anchored. Pictured here is the Union encampment at the lighthouse. (Courtesy of the Library of Congress.)

While the lighthouse was not damaged during these engagements, the Chicamacomico Races compelled a plea to the War Department for adequate protection for the sentinel in order to acquire and ensure the safety of a new lens. Shipwrecks continued to happen. The steamer lantern needed replacement as soon as possible. Seen here is an illustration of the sinking of the USS *Monitor* off Hatteras. (Courtesy of NOAA.)

On March 15, 1862, W.J. Newman, acting engineer, landed at Hatteras to make an assessment of the lighthouse in order to have it relit. He found the lens missing, but the original 1854 external clockwork mechanism and small pedestal remained in place. As the missing lens likely would be found "injured," he suggested installing a new one. Newman discovered that the lighthouse itself needed repairs, calling the tower "obsolete." He felt erecting a new lighthouse might be the most cost effective. Pictured here is the 1870 internal clockwork system and large pedestal manufactured for the modern Cape Hatteras Lighthouse.

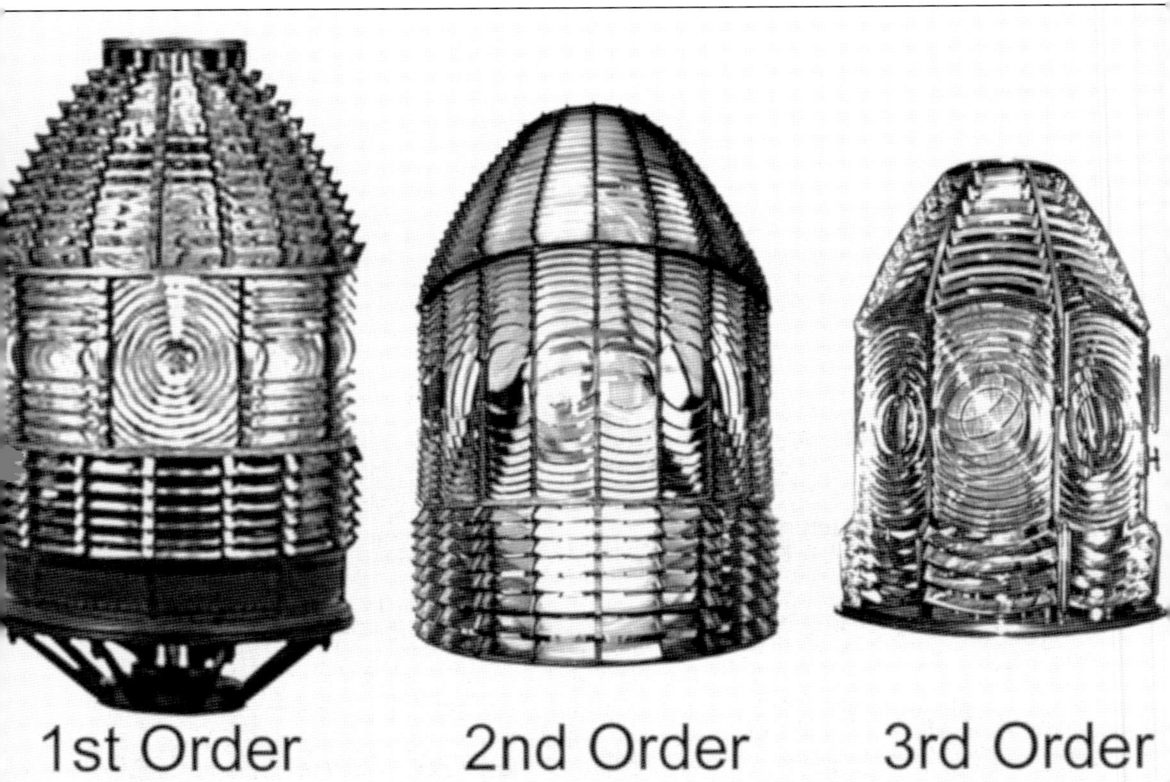

On April 19, 1862, acting engineer W.J. Newman reported that the lighthouse, once lit, might be in danger of attack and requested troops to guard it. Newman heard the original lens was in Tarboro. In May, a second-order Fresnel lens, shown here, was placed in the lighthouse and likely lit around June 1, 1862. The second-order lens was extinguished on June 17, 1863. Shortly after, a "1855 Leparites Moderator Lamp 1st Order" was installed, according to the *Cape Hatteras Lighthouse Historic Structure Report*. In April 1865, the Civil War ended. Within five months, the 1854 lens was discovered by Union patrol at Henderson, North Carolina. It was shipped to the lighthouse depot in Staten Island, New York, then sent to Paris in 1867 for repairs by the Henry-Lepaute Co. (The lens returned to Staten Island for storage in 1868.) In March 1867, money was approved for a new lighthouse at Cape Hatteras. Newman considered his preliminary lighthouse design, costing $88,700, advanced. In October 1868, Dexter Stetson became superintendent of construction. A construction team left for Cape Hatteras to make foundation preparations and collect a shipment of bricks. Delays occurred. On February 19, 1869, the schooner *Ida Nicholson* grounded in a storm several miles from Hatteras Inlet with 101,600 bricks. (Courtesy of the US Lighthouse Society.)

By late March 1869, workers were finished erecting buildings to house employees, a cement house, a kitchen, and a blacksmith shop. They built a wharf on the sound side and laid down a railroad to transport materials from the wharf to the lighthouse. The workers constructed a crane derrick and a cofferdam around the tower site, with the latter affording a pumped-out area that helped provide a dry work environment. Pictured above is the double keepers' quarters.

The 1869 annual report described the lighthouse as being "on the general level as the beach," making it secure from the wind. Descriptions included that the site was "above the highest level of the sea, and so far, removed from the waterline as to render it safe from encroachments of the sea." Pictured here is plate no. 1 of the lighthouse construction drawings, published in 1869.

The foundation materials included yellow pine timber. The workers laid upon it an octagonal foundation of granite blocks placed in cement mortar. The granite foundation was built atop the timber grillage, seen above. The report was complimentary: "When completed it will be the most imposing and substantial brick light-house on this continent, if not in the world." With the base of the structure finished on November 30, 1869, the tower brickwork began. Laborers on the island helped the work move quickly throughout 1870. They were excited to earn up to $1.50 daily. Supplies of bricks and window frame casings arrived as well as iron stairways and stores. Crafts folk created the ironwork at Bartlett, Robbins & Co. in Baltimore, pictured below in an 1873 lithograph. By April 30, the tower was 103 feet from the ground. They installed a new first-order Fresnel lens, which ironically turned out to be the original Fresnel lens from the 1854 tower. A June report stated that the tower was 147 feet from the ground with not "a brick out of line an eighth of an inch." Mid-June saw engineer J.H. Simpson having the Baltimore lantern makers making slight changes to the new lantern to accommodate the old lens. By July, the tower had reached 153.5 feet. But crafting the ironwork alterations for the new lens was taking time, and work was halted. On September 9, 1870, the ironwork shipped aboard *Tulip.* (Below, courtesy of the Baltimore Museum of Industry.)

Building the lighthouse included receiving instructions on caring for the white and black tiling, pictured here, on the tower landings. "To darken and polish the black tiling, rub the planed surface with a rag dipped in Linseed, Lamp or any kind of waste oil; using care that it does not touch the white tiles as it injures their appearance."

Engineer J.H. Simpson gave an annual report in late September on the progress of the lighthouse project. He brought the project up to date and praised the quality of work as "thorough in character" with "brick work laid in the most substantial manner. The structure thus far gives the assurance that it will meet in every respect the anticipations of the L.H. Board." Shown here is original brickwork.

On October 5, 1870, construction of the lighthouse resumed. A November report stated that the main work of building was finished. What remained was setting up of the lantern and lens, finishing work, laying tiling, fitting doors and sashes, glazing, cement and whitewashing, and construction of the iron fence and its granite base. Pictured at the base of the lighthouse is the iron fence.

Lampist George J. Crossman was given instructions on how to install the lens at Cape Hatteras and was assigned to take down the old lens and pack it for shipment as well as accompany it to Tompkinsville, New York. The new lantern and lens were installed in the sentinel, and the light was presented on December 16, 1870. The light in the old beacon was extinguished and the lens removed. Shown here is the lighthouse in 1893.

The former lighthouse was destroyed on February 11, 1871. This 1893 image, taken from the south, is believed to have been photographed from the top of the foundation mound of the first lighthouse. On February 16, 1871, it was announced that the new tower's focal plane height was 190.89 feet. Brick housing for the principal keeper went up. In 1873, the new Cape Hatteras Lighthouse was painted to display her classic black-and-white spiral daymark. From the ground to the top of the pinnacle, the lighthouse stood 198 feet, 2.5 inches. A tablet bearing the name of the station and the date it was built was placed in the lighthouse.

For centuries, the Cape Hatteras lighthouses withstood fires, an earthquake, lightning strikes, hurricanes, and erosion. Storms and lamp oil fires resulted in glass breakage in the lantern. Cracks appeared in the tower due to vibrations during storms. Erosion caused the displacement of sand at the base. Lightning destroyed marble tiles on the first floor. Fortunately, the second assistant keeper who was struck by that lighting survived. An earthquake caused the tower to sway "like a tree shaken by the wind," according to the *Cape Hatteras Lighthouse Historic Structure Report*. During a powerful hurricane in 1899, the tower windows leaked, and the storm vibration caused plaster to break off where the supporting beams to the landing platforms of the stairway met. This image shows the Cape Hatteras Lighthouse and debris from the 1803 lighthouse foundation.

Upgrades and repairs continued throughout the life of the Cape Hatteras Lighthouse. The sentinel was repainted in 1876. With the lightning strike of 1879 came the decision to utilize a metal rod to link the ironwork of the tower with an iron disk buried in the ground. Shown here is a new conduit attached to the 1913 weight system tracks or rails.

In 1881, two sets of first-order hydraulic float lamps were ordered to take the place of the original mechanical lamps. That same year, repairs were made to the keepers' quarters, and it was decided to put in place electric call bells connecting the keepers' quarters to the tower. In 1886, work on the lighthouse windows, lantern, and assistant keepers' quarters was authorized. Pictured here is the new oil house that went up in 1892.

On May 30, 1898, the Cape Hatteras station became telephonically connected to telegraph stations and were equipped to serve as coast signal stations operating with the US Life-Saving Stations in their vicinity. Within two years, the outdated call bell system was replaced by telephones. By 1910, the Bureau of Lighthouses, overseen by the Department of Commerce, replaced the United States Lighthouse Board. Pictured is the Loran Station with the Cape Hatteras Lighthouse in the background.

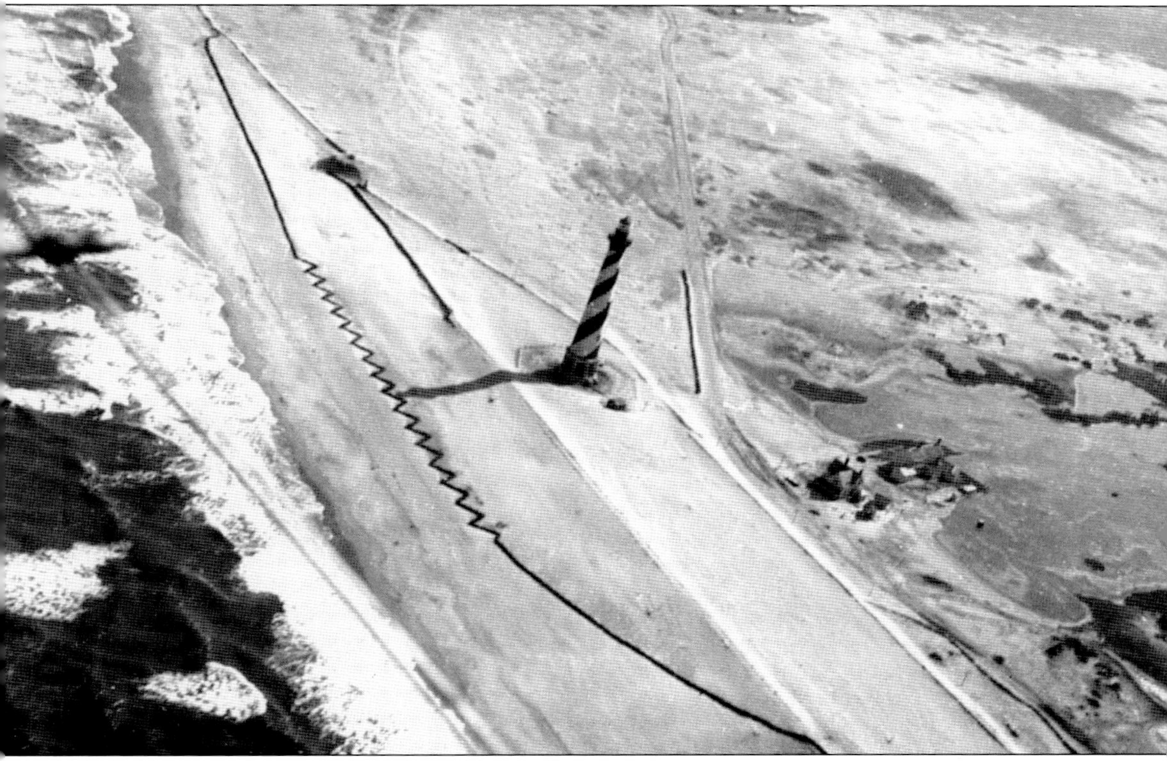

Within three years, the lighthouse's light used an incandescent oil vapor lamp with compressed kerosene in a mantle. In 1930, sheet pile groins were erected in the surf to stave off erosion, seen here. Four years later, the light was electrified, making the manual-operating mechanisms obsolete.

In 1972, the lighthouse gained a new beacon with 800,000 candlepower (focused by two parabolic reflectors) and two 100-watt lamps. The lighthouse can be seen 20 nautical miles in clear weather and flashes every 7.5 seconds. A photocell automatically turns the light on and off. Its rotation is like an airport beacon, and this beacon projects two beams (the 1854 Fresnel lens casts 24). As a safety precaution, a backup bulb and primary reflector automatically turn in place when the principal bulb burns out. The bulbs, made by General Electric, are "halogen/argon filled with a tungsten filament," according to the *Cape Hatteras Lighthouse Historic Structure Report*. The cost for a single replacement bulb—$240—seems high, yet to sailors the lights are invaluable. Seen here is a view of the top of the Cape Hatteras Lighthouse displaying the lighting apparatus and stunning architecture.

Three

Erosion, Vandalism, and a Changing of the Guard

Tending to the Cape Hatteras Lighthouse, shown here in May 1893, was constant and complex, like caring for an infant and an aging grandmother at the same time. Add in weather and there was an ongoing battle that, at times, must have seemed fruitless albeit necessary. In 1893, civil engineer and surveyor Herbert Bamber's survey drawings illustrated that the waterline had moved more than 1,000 feet from the lighthouse.

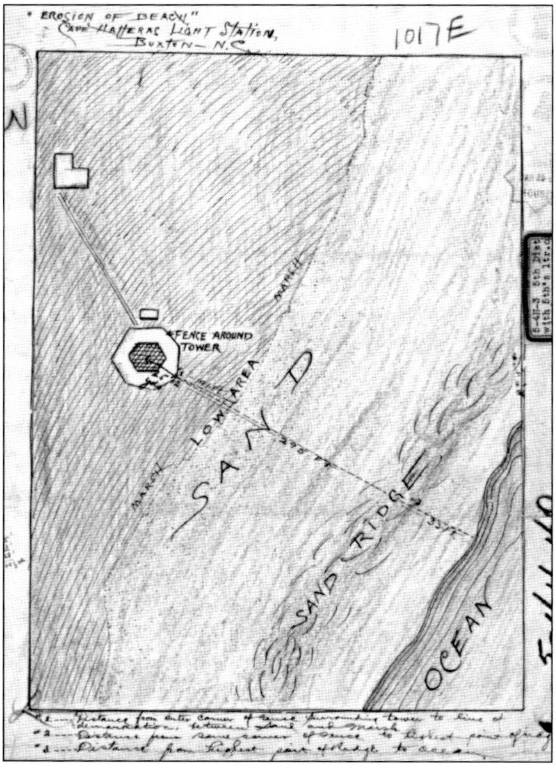

By 1919, the shoreline was approximately 333 feet from the lighthouse, as seen in the c. 1919 drawing depicting the erosion at the light station. In 1924, funds were requested to put toward controlling erosion, but Congress did not respond. However, damage from the hurricane of 1930 resulted in the installation of 900 feet of "interlocking sheet pile groins" along the shore. Unfortunately, the groins did not stop water from reaching within 100 feet of the lighthouse when a Category 3 hurricane hit south of Cape Hatteras. Workers added additional steel groins. As the erosion conflict continued, the Bureau of Lighthouses sought to purchase land to construct a new station. The land they targeted was owned by lighthouse keeper Unaka Jennette. In 1935, he sold the tract for $266,880. The photograph above illustrates the precarious nature of the lighthouse. (Left, courtesy of the Cape Hatteras Light Station, RG 26, National Archives. Copied from Ross Holland Jr.'s "A History of Cape Hatteras Light Station.")

Pictured here are the 150-foot black skeleton tower (right) and tower light (below) that were built on property about 1.5 miles west-northwest from the 1870 sentinel. Completed on September 18, 1935, and lit on May 13, 1936, it demonstrated a 90,000-candlepower flashing light. The sentinel rose above sea level 166 feet and was visible 19 miles out to sea. The 1870 lighthouse light was then extinguished.

A Civilian Conservation Corps (CCC) camp, housing 200 men, was set up on the island about a half mile from the 1870 beacon. The image above shows the barracks in the distance at Camp Diamond Shoals. Workers stabilized the beach, created artificial dunes, and worked to restore the island's indigenous plants such as salt-tolerant grasses. Millions of sea oats were propagated and planted. The CCC also built sand fences and wooden revetments. The fences were set up in front and behind the lighthouse, thereby lowering wind speed and allowing sand to accumulate to form dunes. By 1937, the sand dunes had gained a substantial height. Beach erosion was reduced to some extent. Seen below in this 1938 black-and-white photograph of the Cape Hatteras Lighthouse are stabilizing grasses and newly installed electric poles and lines. In August 1937, Congress passed the bill to establish the Cape Hatteras National Seashore. Pres. Franklin Delano Roosevelt signed the bill authorizing the creation of the first national seashore, dependent upon the contribution of 10,000 acres of land by the state or by a private donor within 10 years. In November, the light station became part of the National Park Service.

In 1939, the CCC started giving tours of the lighthouse. In mid-February 1939, Horace A. Dough was selected to oversee both the Cape Hatteras and Currituck Lighthouse reservations as acting custodian and also became custodian of Kill Devil Hill National Monument. Pictured here in 1934 are Frank Stick, left, and Dough, right. Stick was instrumental in the formation of a national park at Cape Hatteras. He came up with the idea in 1933 and spent nearly 20 years promoting it. He was the secretary of the Cape Hatteras National Seashore Commission.

A 1939 site plan illustrated how much the Atlantic Ocean had moved toward the light station from 1852 to 1872—720 feet. Between 1872 and 1937, it had moved 1,420 feet closer. By 1939, the sentinel was about 600 feet from the sea. The same year, in preparation for World War II, the United States Light House Service went under the authority of the Coast Guard. By March 31, 1940, the CCC's Diamond Shoals camp was closed. The lighthouse is shown here not far from the surf.

About three months later, the park gained a new designation—Cape Hatteras National Seashore Recreational Area. The National Park Service developed parking and added restrooms. A recommendation came that the lighthouse and park be designated a national historic site as part of the Cape Hatteras National Seashore Recreational Area. In 1942, following America's entry into World War II, the Coast Guard leased the lighthouse as a watchtower for spotting U-boats that had been wreaking havoc on shipping lanes by sinking vessels. The idea surfaced to reestablish the Cape Hatteras Lighthouse. On March 18, 1942, U-124 torpedoed the tanker *Papoose*, seen below, as the Allied vessel ran close to shore in a blacked-out state while passing Diamond Shoals. (Below, courtesy of the Mariners Museum and Park.)

In September 1943, a request to reestablish the light was generated by lighthouse inspector Lt. Comdr. F. Phippany. He gave a relatively good report of the 1870 tower and proposed relighting it as it was closer to the Coast Guard station than the steel tower. Phippany reasserted his request in October 1944, but even his report of vandals harming the 1870s sentinel did not convince his superiors, who were concerned with erosion. Erosion was evidenced by that September's Great Atlantic Hurricane, which set back headway the CCC made. Seen here are upper dioptric and catadioptric prism panels removed from the lighthouse around 1949.

Old Lighthouse Outwits Storms But Not Thieves

BUXTON, N. C.—(INS)—Cape Hatteras lighthouse, the oldest in America, was prey last night for thieves.

The lighthouse which has withstood the hazards of war, storms, and hurricanes galore, is reported damaged by vandals who crawled to the top of its 192-foot tower.

Two heavy padlocks installed by the coast guard within the past 15 months have been removed from atop the tower.

Capt. N. C. Manyon, of the lighthouse service, said that a resident guard may be assigned to protect the oldest and tallest lighthouse in America, abandoned 14 years ago.

At that time, it seemed inevitable that the tower would survive. It was expected to topple in the ocean.

Vandalism to the lighthouse continued. A 1946 report was bleak: windowpanes smashed and glass lens prisms taken out. Pictured at left is a newspaper clipping reporting the break-in. Horace A. Dough suggested that the Coast Guard return custody of the lighthouse to the National Park Service and help restore it to the condition it was in before they took it over at the start of 1942. A battle ensued with the Coast Guard asserting that it had done the best it could during wartime. The Coast Guard permit expired on August 15, 1947, and the National Park Service took over the lighthouse. Arguments continued. Except for providing more security, little was done for the lighthouse up to early 1948. In the spring, the Coast Guard filed for a special use permit to use the lighthouse primarily as an aid to the movement of ships. The Coast Guard tried to find a replacement Fresnel lens, but the group was unsuccessful and suggested using a modern lens, to which the National Park Service eventually agreed. The National Park Service filed reports in June and October 1948. The NPS recorded that machinery parts were missing and prisms broken or gone. One planner called the site a "disgrace." Pictured below is the lighthouse in 1948. (Left, courtesy of the *Tennessean*, March 9, 1947, newspapers.com.)

After meeting with the NPS in November 1948, the Coast Guard agreed to make repairs. In 1949, it painted the inside and outside of the structure, restored windows, and erected a chain-link fence around the oil house and lighthouse to keep out vandals. The Coast Guard packed up the remnants of the Fresnel lens to be placed in storage. Seen above are upper dioptric and catadioptric prism panels. The lens was supposed to be replaced with an historic lens, but the Coast Guard did not accomplish that. The NPS and Coast Guard conversed about repairing the lens, but reports came in that spare parts were not available and the cost to have them manufactured was too high. An agreement came about for the Coast Guard to take responsibility for the care of the historic structure. The Coast Guard upgraded the beloved lighthouse to include the installation of commercial power lines. And, finally, a new 40-inch Corning Glass Works lens, which radiated three times the light of the former lens, was put in place. Pictured at right is the duplex lens assembly. The automatic light worked by using a Swedish-built clock to control it. The light in the 1870 Cape Hatteras Lighthouse was relit on January 23, 1950. Tower visitation was offered to visitors. If not for the erosion control efforts made in the 1930s, which extended the coastline, the lighthouse likely would not have been activated.

After years of intense planning and negotiations regarding the formal establishment of the Cape Hatteras National Seashore Recreational Area, in 1953 the director of the NPS recommended that the federal government "approve an order, consistent with Section 4 of the Act of August 17, 1937, directing that certain lands on the Outer Banks of North Carolina be administered, protected, and developed by the National Park Service for national seashore recreational purposes for the benefit and enjoyment of the people." January 12 is the designated anniversary of this outcome. The NPS took steps to understand the task of managing an ever-changing national resource. And that same year, visitors began to climb the lighthouse. A study of cultural and natural features of the seashore began in August 1954 to research changes related to vegetation, storms, and geology regarding the drifting Outer Banks. The study resulted in two publications to aid park management. The undertaking was both challenging and complex as it not only dealt with human impact on the park, but also the unending toll nature presented. Seen here is a spacious view of the lighthouse site in 1955.

Hurricanes continued to hit the Atlantic coast, including Hazel in October 1954 and Connie in 1955. A 10-year program—Mission 66—began February 2, 1956, for capital improvements to the weathered park infrastructure. The focus was to first control erosion. The list included maintaining the dunes and their breaches that allowed vegetation to wash away. The park needed to be user friendly by providing places to drive, park, walk, and explore without inundating a single area with a mass of people. By mid-October, the Dune Construction and Beach Rehabilitation Project was launched. Pictured here is Allyn F. Hanks, the first superintendent of the seashore (1954–1957).

The Cape Hatteras National Seashore was dedicated on April 24, 1958. Several ceremonies occurred. The ceremony for dedicating the Cape Hatteras National Seashore Recreational Area was held at the lighthouse visitor center. This included unveiling a plaque honoring the late Henry Phipps, who had made the first donation to the project; his family had donated 2,700 acres of land to the national seashore. The plaque hangs in the entranceway to the double keepers' quarters. Phipps's grandson Raymond R. Guest (above left), pictured with Gov. Luther Hodges, stands next to the dedication plaque. Guest was a second cousin of Winston Churchill. Pictured below, the dedication included a "mixing of the waters" from the Old Faithful geyser and the Atlantic Ocean by Superintendent Gibbs and Coast Guard general H.C. Moore at Coquina Beach. Shown are, from left to right, former superintendent Hanks, Governor Hodges, Superintendent Gibbs, Admiral Moore, director Wirth (at speaker's podium), former representative Lindsay Warren, Rep. Herbert C. Bonner, Assistant Secretary of Interior Roger Ernst, and Clark Stratton.

Despite hard work, storms continued to take their toll, including Hurricane Helene, which in 1958 destroyed a new road and downed sand fencing. In 1960, Hurricane Donna damaged park roads, buildings, and vegetation. The Ash Wednesday Storm of March 1962 caused the relocation of park headquarters from Bodie Island to Manteo. Four years later, the NPS placed 312,000 cubic yards of sand taken from the sound to the beach in front of the beacon. The sand was too fine and washed away. In 1970, the hardening of the coast with groins to protect the US Navy facility north of the lighthouse accelerated erosion south of the facility. Three groins projecting seaward are shown in this image. A second beach renourishment occurred the following winter, but it was too small to have any real impact.

In 1973, a total of 1.25 million cubic yards of sand was placed 3,500 feet north of the lighthouse and stretched northward for 1.5 miles, widening the beach by 300–350 feet. Pictured above is a beach renourishment project in action, and below is the machinery used in the effort. An alternative to continual efforts to curb erosion came in 1974: Move the lighthouse. David Clary, with the Office of Archaeology and Historic Preservation, wrote: "A pure naturalist might argue in reply that historical tradition would be best saved by allowing the lighthouse to fall into the sea. When professional emotions are set aside, however, the dilemma turns out to be an economic one. What will it cost to move the lighthouse?" It was recommended that a study be done to answer that question. By 1975, the lighthouse was 175 feet from the beach, and it was closed due to cracks in its structure. The date of reopening was not known, according to the National Park Service.

A study in 1977 noted critical rusting and cracking of the lighthouse's brackets. NPS recommended an "installation of an external tie-band around and through the brackets." In 1978, high tides were causing challenges for remnants of the 1803 lighthouse foundation, seen here. In March 1980, a nor'easter washed away what remained. This constant battle called for action by the fall; the southern shoreline was within 70 feet of the lighthouse. The NPS took interim measures to extend the southernmost groin. A study seeking solutions to save the lighthouse resulted in these suggestions: "Moving the structure, constructing a full revetment, constructing a partial revetment with new groins, and beach nourishment, the installation of new groins with beach nourishment, and only beach nourishment."

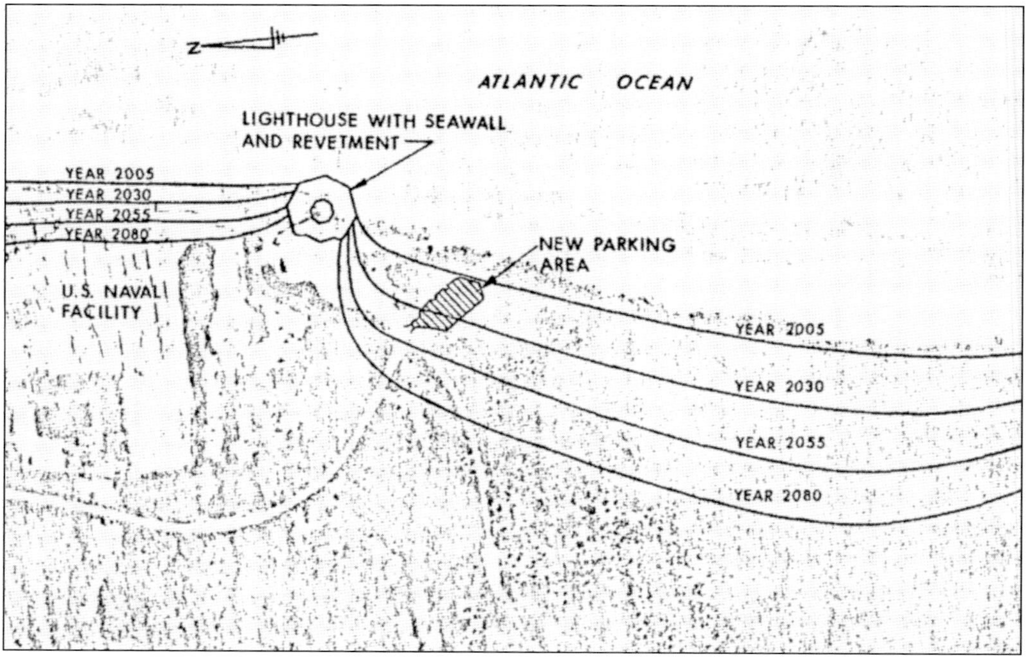

A fascinating temporary protection proposal came when it was suggested to install SEASCAPE, artificial seaweed made of polypropylene fabric. The seaweed would slow down the speed of the sand-bearing currents, allowing sand to build up around the artificial seaweed. The first installation sequence was completed in May 1981. It significantly built up the beach south of the southern groin. That same year, the Army Corps of Engineers (ACOE) and the National Park Service joined forces regarding erosion challenges at the lighthouse. By the end of the year, the ACOE introduced two alternatives (diagrams shown here) to provide long-term security: a seawall revetment around the lighthouse and building multiple "inshore breakwaters" on the lighthouse coastline.

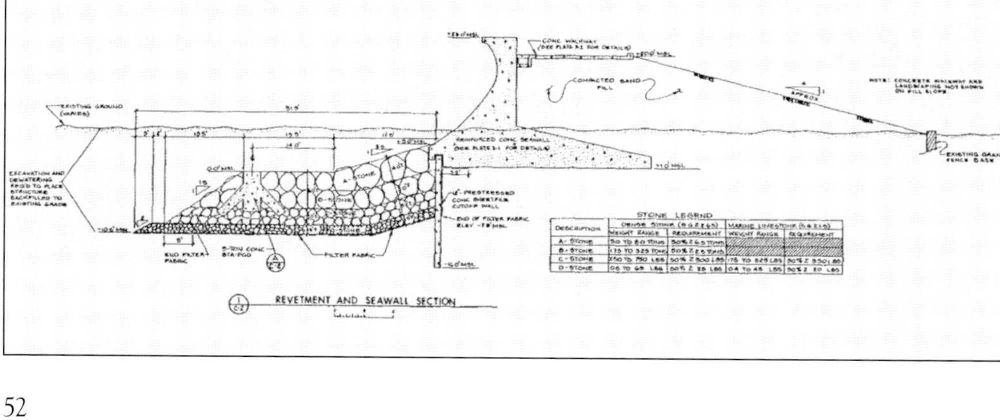

It was not just the powers that be who were concerned with protecting the lighthouse. In 1982, Hugh Morton, a North Carolina developer and photographer, started a statewide "Save the Lighthouse" campaign. Children gave their precious coins, while corporations made generous donations. State government joined the effort by backing the campaign. Workshops and meetings were held, and ideas proposed. The most popular public opinion was to build a seawall revetment. In the meantime, to ready for the winter season, around 700 sandbags were positioned around the lighthouse, and more artificial seaweed was installed. It could not be concluded, though, that the seaweed was helping due to accretion of shore north and south of the lighthouse. In fact, some of the units were breaking up due to turbulent surf. Temporary measures also included putting a scour mat apron in place around the foot of the southern groin. Pictured here is an example of sandbags installed earlier in Buxton.

The following year, a report from the National Park Service Southeast Regional Office was authored by the University of Virginia and titled *Coastal Erosion at Cape Hatteras: A Lighthouse in Danger.* It concluded: "Without a major engineering effort to protect it, the Cape Hatteras Lighthouse will soon be destroyed by an encroaching sea. Considering the cost of this protection, an inventory of other Atlantic coast structures under similar threat should be made before other protection projects are undertaken. We can only afford to save the most valuable property. The Cape Hatteras Lighthouse may well stand out as a notable example of the dangers of construction on barrier islands where the erosion rates are large and variable." Pictured here is an image of the Cape Hatteras Lighthouse that clearly illustrates the peril that existed from the advancing sea.

The main gallery and its supporting structure needed work. The NPS advertised for the job, but all proposals were greater than the allocated funds. Meanwhile, the 1984 General Management Plan (GMP) for the park, recognizing the need to protect historic assets, also realized that fighting erosion was pointless and recommended that the destiny of the lighthouse not be determined solely by the plan. The report stressed the need for permanent protection; a commitment to preserving the cultural resources of the barrier island, especially those relating to humans' adaptation to the coastal environment; to stop stabilization efforts; and to work to establish the "light station complex a Historic Zone." In the end, the National Park Service was committing to preserving and protecting the historic and archaeological resources for eternity. This photograph captures the majesty of the 1980 Cape Hatteras Lighthouse keepers' quarters as well as the jetty in the surf.

The lighthouse closed in the fall of 1984 after a 40-pound portion of metal trim fell from the structure, probably a result of Hurricane Diana striking in September 1984. A year later, Hurricane Gloria hit Hatteras Island blowing 100 knots. Pictured here is an aerial view of storm overwash with Cape Hatteras Lighthouse in the background. In the spring of 1985, the NPS finished the last parameters for the seawall revetment project. The lighthouse remained closed until 1994.

By November, the long-term protection design was complete. The seawall/revetment would be octagonal in shape and surround the lighthouse with a section facing land open to guests. The scheduled completion date was February 1988. The plan had four primary components: a concrete seawall, a sheet pile cutoff wall, a stone revetment, and a compacted earth fill, according to the *Cape Hatteras Lighthouse Historic Structure Report*. The cost was $5.575 million. Seen here is a seawall protecting the Cape Hatteras Lighthouse.

A detailed examination of the lighthouse resulted in a report coming out in March 1986. Hasbrouck, Hunderman Architects and Wiss, Janney, Elstner Associates Inc. studied the structure from the granite base to the watch room. The report noted every challenge, from thermal expansion cracks in the walls to missing hardware on bronze doors. Seen here is a partial view of the entrance with the lighthouse disappearing into the sky.

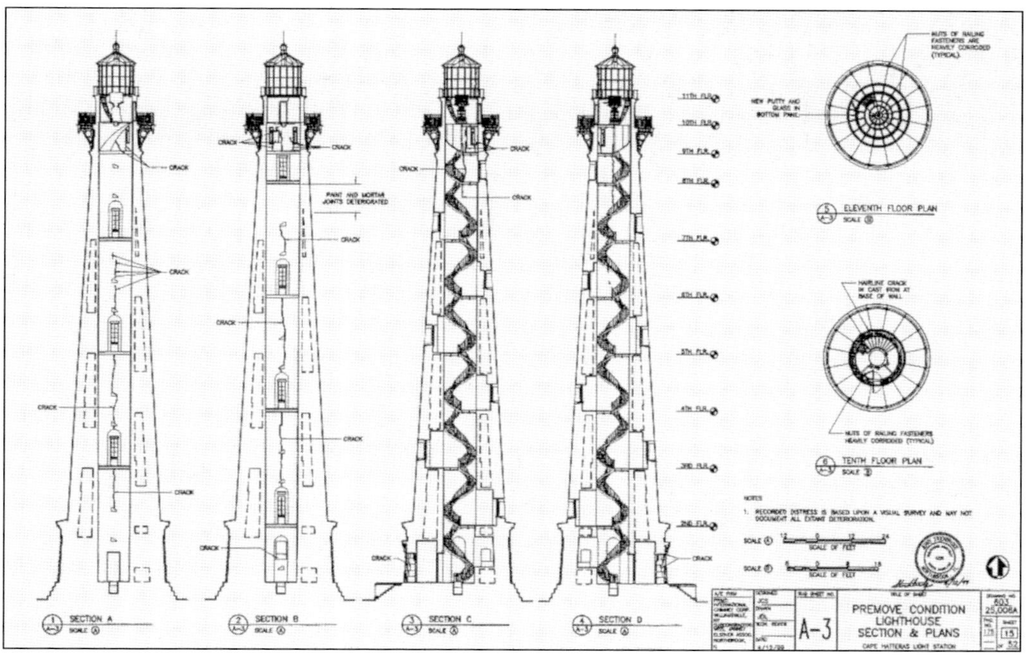

A second report in 1986 defined the "critical" and "serious" priorities. It also included a suggested maintenance and long-term conservation plan. Ever faithful to its mission to protect and preserve the lighthouse, the National Park Service called upon the National Academy of Sciences (NAS) for a review on how to best meet its goal. This drawing shows the pre-move condition of the lighthouse.

A committee formed on "Options for Preserving Cape Hatteras Lighthouse" with the National Research Council and National Academy of Sciences joining forces. Their job was to name and evaluate preservation options with an eye on protection, cost, risks, and impact on visitors and the environment. This included evaluating the seawall revetment project and restoring the groin field without a revetment or with a partial one. They weighed the pros and cons and decided that the best option was to relocate the lighthouse, citing these reasons: "Minimal risk of damage to lighthouse during implementation, reliable long-term solution, little impact on historic and visual integrity, few adverse environmental impacts, few conflicts of governmental policies, lower initial cost with no other risk-related maintenance costs." Seen here is an image of the vulnerable yet elegant Cape Hatteras Lighthouse.

Four

The Move of the Century

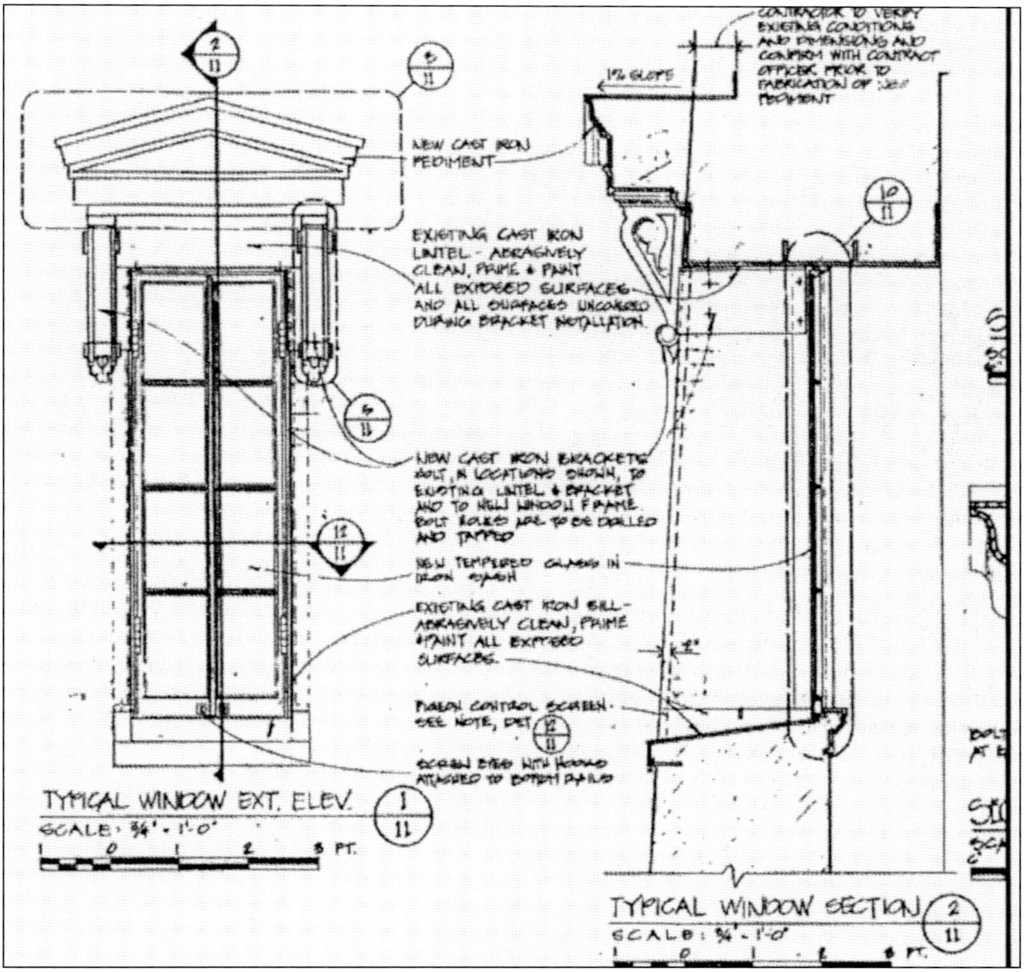

Until a decision came about, work on the lighthouse would cease, though drawings for preserving the lighthouse were finished in March 1988 and revised in October the following year. The plan called for more than 100 cast-iron fabrications related to everything from gallery support brackets and gridwork to window pediments and stair treads. Seen here are details for the preservation of the exterior windows and the hoods.

As caretakers for a coastal lighthouse in peril, the National Park Service must have been exhausted from attending meetings, requesting and examining reports, and shouldering the sheer responsibility of protecting a beloved historic site that had been basically threatened since its creation. Still in the planning process but close to a solution, the NPS weighed all protection possibilities against "the National Historic Protection Act of 1966, the National Environmental Policy Act of 1969, the Coastal Barriers Resources Act of 1982, the National Flood Insurance Act of 1968," and others. In August 1988, the park service recommended relocation approximately "2,900 feet to the southwest and 1,500 feet from the shoreline." The plan was for all historic structures to keep to the same original arrangement as the old site. New additions included parking, restroom and shower facilities, and beach access. Also included was restoration of the groin field to protect the lighthouse until the move. Pictured here is the original layout of buildings on the site.

Moving the lighthouse was becoming a reality. Work began on examining the proposed path and what was needed to shore it up to withstand the weight of its precious cargo. This included designing a method of movement and a foundation surface for the track. In April 1989, the NPS released a new report that included the price of the project—$8.775 million, including planning and construction costs, new site development, interpretation, and existing site reclamation. Public feedback was divided, yet the plan met with approval in late October 1989. The National Park Service stated that "the move will not be implemented until the risk of loss by erosion or rise in sea level equals or exceeds the risk of loss by a move, and until Congress has provided adequate funding." Pictured here is a bird's-eye view of the Cape Hatteras Lighthouse with the jetty wall.

In 1990, the International Chimney Corporation (ICC) received a $946,380 contract to restore and ready the lighthouse for the demanding relocation. The National Park Service determined what was necessary to make the move, and a team formed to create a request for proposals. A report, *The Relocation of the Cape Hatteras Lighthouse: A Potential Optional Relocation Method that Illustrates our Project Approach, i.e., the Analysis of Potential Optional Methods*, divided the move into two parts: the base and the main body. The outline included preparing the route, creating and building the runway, shoring up the lighthouse structure, creating a protection structure for around the lighthouse, moving both onto the runway, building a new foundation, pulling the lighthouse, removing and relocating the base, installing the lighthouse on the base, removing preparatory parts used to shore up the lighthouse, and restoring masonry. Pictured here are sandbags protecting the Cape Hatteras Lighthouse.

In 1992, work included creating a contract to restore the compromised sandbag revetment, awarding a contract to create a new lighthouse site, negotiating relocation specifications, reviewing beach erosion and the potential risks to the lighthouse, and temporary protection recommendations. A start-up report was submitted for moving the lighthouse, which confirmed the development program and "establishment of the project approach and the continuation on to the separate 'Lighthouse Move Project,' " according to the park's *Cape Hatteras Lighthouse Historic Structure Report*. On August 8, 1993, Hurricane Emily made landfall near Hatteras, blowing 100 knots. The National Park Service scavenged to find materials, including loose stone, to protect the lighthouse. That year, the park service's southeast regional director requested a temporary halt to the "contract for development of the relocation specifications." The NPS felt that those funds were needed for emergency purposes. The year 1994 would also see the repair of the south groin. By late 1993, the International Chimney Corporation lighthouse restoration work was finished. Yet a hurricane swept in and damaged lantern windows and part of the handrail. The International Chimney Corporation repaired the damage by the spring of 1994. Pictured here is a 1991 aerial view of the lighthouse.

After receiving $10,000 from the Save the Lighthouse Committee, the International Chimney Corporation repaired the lighthouse roof. The tower, pictured here, was painted and opened for climbing in the spring of 1994. The park superintendent proclaimed that "the risk of leaving the lighthouse where it was outweighed the risk of moving it." A request came to add a fourth groin southward as part of a three-step preservation plan that also included putting in place sandbags and moving the lighthouse. The North Carolina Natural Resources Commission denied the request. The denial was made public, which motivated elected state officials to jump onboard the relocation train.

The North Carolina Senate president pro tempore, Marc Basnight, requested that a committee of professors from North Carolina State University examine the 1988 NAS study. In January 1997, they concluded not only that the lighthouse should move, but that it occur posthaste to achieve the needed funding. Basnight also received the support of Pres. Bill Clinton, who passed the assignment to his chief of staff, Erskine Bowles. Additional support from US senator Lauch Faircloth, seen below, resulted in a $2 million appropriation in 1998, which allowed the National Park Service to begin seeking and granting a design/build contract. North Carolina's congressional delegation and state leaders were divided, with Faircloth and Gov. James Hunt in favor and Sen. Jesse Helms and Rep. Walter Jones opposed. Basnight, a Manteo native, initially supported relocation but later backed Dare County in opposing the move. Pictured at right is the Cape Hatteras Lighthouse before it was moved in 1999.

While several factions were moving forward laying the groundwork to move the lighthouse, another group was having second thoughts. State representative Walter Jones went from supporting the move to siding with his Buxton supporters who were against the move. As a result, a public hearing was held on April 9, 1998, and both sides were presented. A representational speaker relayed Gov. James Hunt's support for the move. Within six months, $9.8 million was committed by Congress for the relocation. The International Chimney Incorporated (ICC) received the contract due to its technology and knowledge of the lighthouse. Pictured at left is the Cape Hatteras Lighthouse. In January 1999, work began to carefully deconstruct the site to prepare for excavation, take precautionary measures to ensure the safety of the structure, and supply a clear moving path. Steps included recording, labeling, and removing the granite footers for the original 1871 iron fence, walkway, entrance stairs, and their foundation. Trees were cleared from the intended pathway. The road had to be prepared, which included grading, covering with gravel, tamping, and rolling to prep the pathway to receive the steel beam mat necessary to accommodate the moving lighthouse. Pictured below is the oil house making its inaugural move in February.

The *Cape Hatteras Lighthouse Historic Structure Report* records an historic moment: "On February 13, a diamond-tipped cable saw began cutting through the foundation between the fourth and fifth plinth courses. As a portion of the plinth was cut apart, workers would then use pneumatic air hammers and chisels to chip away at the granite rubble foundation held together with cement mortar." Pictured here is the original foundation.

Come March, the team set its sights on the principal keepers' and double keepers' quarters. This included working on the replacement foundations. A tractor trailer moved the dwellings between March 24 and March 26. Pictured here is the moving of the principal keepers' quarters (above) and the double keepers' quarters (below).

Despite years of caretaking, cutting into the foundation felt like a defining action. The workers removed a section of it and put steel mats in place. They placed steel shoring towers with feet jacks underneath, with steel beams above for support between the mats below and plinth above, according to the *Cape Hatteras Lighthouse Historic Structure Report*. Section by section, the crew continued the process until the lighthouse was supported with the interim shoring towers, seen at right.

The new foundation was in the works. Workers completed the excavation, created formwork, set a giant pattern of rebar, and poured concrete, as seen here. The foundation was backfilled upon the curation of the cement. Deconstruction work continued at the old site with separation and removal of the foundation from the plinth, removal of lateral cross braces in the shoring towers, and the positioning of 70-foot-long primary beams between the shoring towers, according to the *Cape Hatteras Lighthouse Historic Structure Report*.

Workers put the main beams in place on hydraulic jacks with rollers. Pictured here is the first main beam about to be installed. Additional shoring up was done with strongback beams, which held the entire steel support system together. They pressurized the hydraulic jacks upon completion of the support system. The steel network was pushed against the bottom of the sentinel to lift it five feet, four inches. A unified jacking system would lift the lighthouse approximately one inch a minute. The workers added wood cribbing under the primary beams (pictured here) and every foot until they reached the needed height.

The day finally arrived. On June 17, the Cape Hatteras Lighthouse was moved 10 feet, 6 inches. The lighthouse could only be moved five feet "before the rams became fully extended," according to the *Cape Hatteras Lighthouse Historic Structure Report*. Once the structure met the end of the steel mats, the move halted to relocate the mats to the front of the line. The photograph at right shows the lighthouse on June 24. It had been moved 625 feet. Seen below is another view of the move.

The lighthouse's final move came on July 9. It moved just under 80 feet that day. The sentinel needed its foundation. The last section of shoring towers had to be removed and replaced with brick masonry. The lighthouse was lowered onto its new foundation via the jacking system. Seen here are the jacks resting on the cribbing and the park service crossing sign. The sign was signed by everyone involved in the move and is displayed at the Keepers Quarters Move exhibit.

The new elevation was two feet higher, affording protection against erosion and flooding. The new height also allowed the light to be seen farther out to sea. The NPS completed the final inspection on October 1. The chief of interpretation, Bob Woody, seen above left, helped lay the final bricks in the new foundation. Then it was time for a ceremony, pictured below on the evening of November 13, 1999, to relight the lighthouse. The cost of the move totaled $9,518,042, including design work, the relocation, new building foundations, a lighthouse lighting protection system, short-term electrical service, a public viewing area, and disposal services.

The momentous project garnered accolades, including having the Cape Hatteras Lighthouse designated an Historic Civil Engineering Landmark by the American Society of Civil Engineers. It also received the Outstanding Civil Engineering Award from the American Society of Civil Engineers for a "project that best illustrates superior civil engineering skills and represents a significant contribution to civil engineering progress and society." The society cited that the "outstanding team effort between ICC, Expert House Movers, the National Park Service, and others deserved recognition." Pictured here is the Cape Hatteras Lighthouse in its new location.

By August 2000, workers completed the advancement of the new site and redevelopment of the former site. Following this was the opening of the lighthouse to climbers. But as expected, additions, repairs, replacements, and updates continued to the site and sentinel over time. Due to repairs to the interior spiral stairs, the lighthouse was closed beginning June 11, 2001, until 2003. In September 2002, part of the original gallery deck and railing and the first-order Fresnel lens went on loan for display by the Graveyard of the Atlantic Museum in Hatteras Village. After receiving a fresh coat of paint, the lighthouse was reopened on April 18, 2003. Seen here is a view of the landscape from the top of the balcony looking northeast.

In 2005, the Graveyard of the Atlantic Museum financed a project to restore the 1854 lens. Three men, lead lampist Jim Woodward, lampist Jim Dunlap, and jeweler Kurt Fosburg, moved lens parts from a National Park Service storage facility to the museum. In December, the Graveyard of the Atlantic Museum requested the park service loan the pedestal to the museum and was willing to pay for its removal. The NPS agreed to the loan, which also would include other lens panels and railing parts for restoration purposes. The clockwork mechanism and pedestal rejoined the lens in 2006. Pictured here is the restored lens. While the 1854 Cape Hatteras Lighthouse Fresnel lens underwent conservation, it was missing multiple prisms due to vandalism and theft during the period when the lighthouse was unguarded. It is hoped that a future "lens drive" will encourage those who took them as souvenirs to return them to the National Park Service, and they will ultimately be refitted into the still stunning 1854 first-order Fresnel lens. (Courtesy of the North Carolina Department of Natural and Cultural Resources, Department of Archives and History.)

Five

THE LUMINOSITY OF GENIUS

One of the most important figures in the Cape Hatteras Lighthouse story is Augustin-Jean Fresnel (Frĕh-nel), whose design resulted in the lens that was installed in both the 1854 and 1870 lighthouses. Born in Broglie, Normandy, in 1788, Fresnel showed early signs of genius. He went on to become an engineer for France in the Department of Bridges and Roads. Pictured here is an image of Augustin-Jean Fresnel. (Courtesy of the US Lighthouse Society.)

After meeting French mathematician and physicist Francois Arago, seen above, Fresnel experimented on diffraction, polarization of light, wave theory, and optics. His discoveries were met with favor by Arago, who worked for the Académie des sciences. In 1818, Fresnel wrote a memoir on the diffraction of light. It won him the "grand prize in diffraction from the Académie in 1819" (per the *Cape Hatteras Historic Structure Report*) and, subsequently, appointment to the French Lighthouse Commission. Fresnel found current reflectors faulty because mirrors were poor reflective surfaces, "a parabolic form was hard to perfect, a reflector required a hole through it for the lamp, and half of the light source was lost by absorption," he determined according to the *Cape Hatteras Lighthouse Historic Structure Report*. Fresnel positioned a lens in front of one light source to promote refraction, which directed all source light into a beam. He needed to use angled prism glass to get enough light. Manufacturing them was the next step. In time, the prototype was ready. He presented his dioptric lens in 1821. Fresnel then created the catadioptric apparatus. Utilizing the refracting dioptric lenses and the reflecting catadioptric lenses jointly, they could use all the emanating light source. The beacon at Cordouan, seen at right, had the honor of receiving the first Fresnel lens. In 1827, Augustin-Jean Fresnel, 39, succumbed to tuberculosis. Despite his brief life, Fresnel radically changed lighthouse lens technology. (Above left, courtesy of the National Portrait Gallery; above right, courtesy of the US Lighthouse Society.)

A first-order Fresnel lens generally is 12 feet high and more than 6 feet in diameter. The 1854 LePaute first-order Fresnel lens used 1,008 prisms. A 1900s report noted that a first-order Fresnel lens of the time weighed 12,787 pounds and cost $12,500. Pictured here are the six Fresnel lens sizes. The dioptric lens is labeled as the central refracting panels, and the catadioptric lenses are identified as the upper and lower reflecting panels, according to the *Cape Hatteras Lighthouse Historic Structure Report*. (Courtesy of the US Lighthouse Society.)

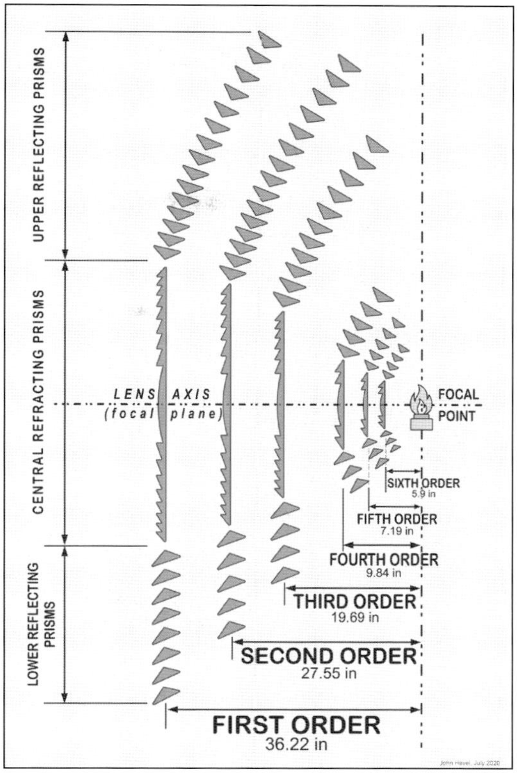

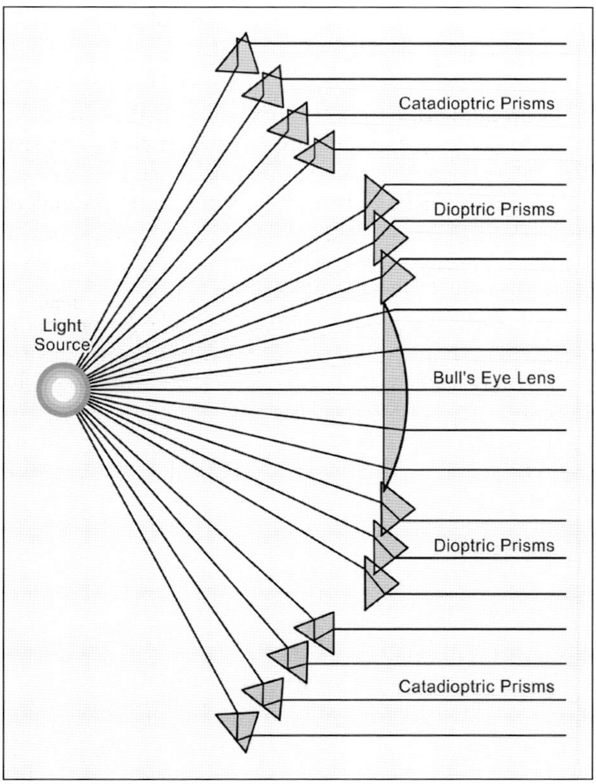

The first-order Fresnel lens used at the Cape Hatteras Lighthouse consisted of 72 panels within a bronze frame network. Placed in three stacks, there were 24 upper catadioptric prisms, 24 central flash panels, and 24 lower catadioptric prisms. Arranged in a circle, they resembled a beehive. Like a mirror, they bent light by reflection. This drawing from the historic Point Reyes Lighthouse shows how a Fresnel lens works. Light was bent from the source into perfectly parallel beams through prisms; dioptric prisms bent the light once, catadioptric prisms bent the light twice. (Courtesy of the US Lighthouse Society.)

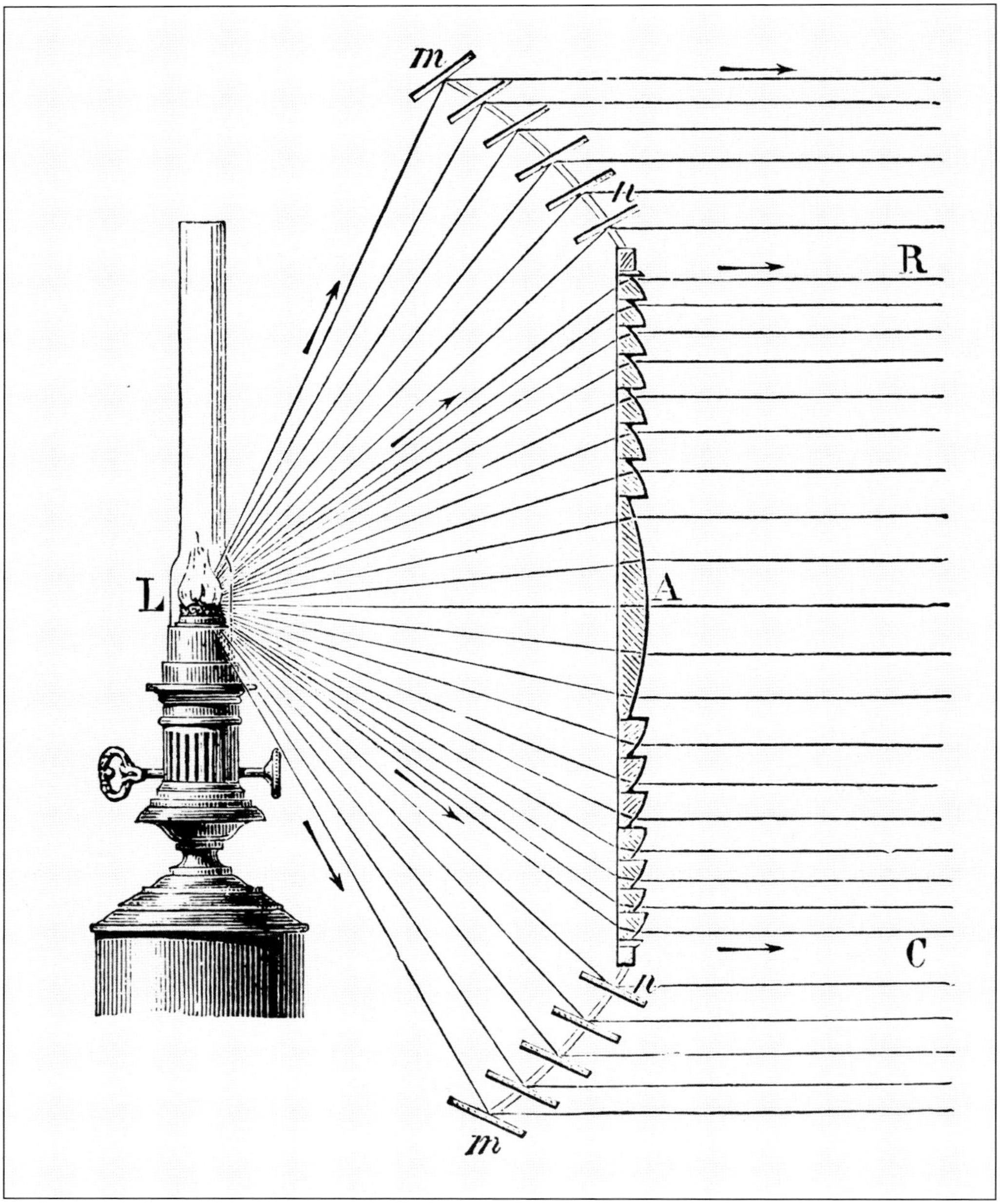

The middle section panels, with bull's-eye lenses, are flash panels. As the lens turns, the concentrated beams from the bull's-eye lenses appear as a flash to the watching sailor. The timing of the motion of the lens is such so that the bull's-eye panel will go past when it is time for a scheduled flash. Located above and below the bull's-eye lenses are dioptric prisms, seen here, that concentrate light like a magnifying glass followed by the lower stacks of catadioptric prisms. Depending on the revolution speed of the lens and the number of flash panels, lighthouses have unique light patterns. The flash panels' lenses, also seen here, provided a unique and identifying flash pattern for the 1854 Hatteras beacon. (Courtesy of the US Lighthouse Society.)

The first-order Fresnel lens assembly in the 1854 lighthouse turned on a chariot at ½ rpm, seen above. It rotated using three 150-pound iron weights that hung from a cable and dropped down 160 feet through the center of the lighthouse into the pedestal to a sand pit, seen below. Like a grandfather clock, the cable wrapped around a drum in the clockwork mechanism under the lens. As the mechanism rotated the lens around the lamp, a flash occurred. Every morning, keepers of the 1854 lighthouse cranked the weights to the top and let them go at dusk upon lighting the lamp. This caused the lens to turn. The gears in the mechanism lent the needed leverage to rotate the one-ton lamp/lens apparatus. A fan governor in the mechanism controlled the rotation speed. A gentle push set the mechanism in motion. It stopped when the weights reached the bottom. The clock ran 15 to 18 hours. (Above, courtesy of John Havel; below, courtesy of the North Carolina Department of Natural and Cultural Resources, Archives and History Department, John Havel photographer.)

Keepers used a variety of oils to light the Cape Hatteras Lighthouse's lantern until electrification in 1934. Initially, they burned whale oil but eventually phased it out due to overhunting. Pictured here is a spermaceti press used to retrieve oil. Colza oil, made from rapeseed, was considered to light the lamp, but it was not a profitable crop. They experimented with porpoise oil, but it was unsuitable. They used kerosene as late as 1927. (Courtesy of the NOAA Photo Library.)

Six

Keeping Watch

The Outer Banks was not a mecca for jobs in the early years. It was considered an honor to be a keeper despite the low pay. At first, keepers with political ties were appointed, but that did not mean they had what it took to do the job. In time, though, it was clear that for safety reasons changes needed to be made, and by 1852, stricter rules were put into place regarding keeper jobs. After that move, keepers were said to be "hardworking and dedicated." Pictured here is the double principal keepers' quarters.

Records, though incomplete, show that the yearly salaries for the principal keepers grew over time, from $333 in 1802 to $800 in 1919. From 1803 until the last keeper was employed, there were a total of 83 keepers at the Cape Hatteras Lighthouse with some men doing more than one stint. Depending on the size of the lighthouse, a site could have as many as five keepers. At first there was only a single, primary keeper on-site at Cape Hatteras. In 1854, the United States Lighthouse Board appointed an assistant lightkeeper. In 1870, a second assistant started work. A third assistant came on board in 1878. But not every year had the same number of assistants. Still, keepers performed all duties because life depended on it despite the number of people employed. Keepers, including the principal keeper, divided all jobs evenly. The Cape Hatteras principal keepers' tours of duty ranged anywhere from 4 months to 18 years depending on a variety of factors such as death, reassignment, release from duty, and resignations. Pictured here is the principal keepers' quarters.

Keepers received a set of instructions that outlined the official duties they were expected to perform. It is impossible to say what task was the most important, for, like a complex clock mechanism, every part had to be "well-oiled" daily. The keepers acted as ambassadors to guests, mechanics, landscapers, painters, guardians, lifesavers, and clerks. Rules included everything from being polite to visitors to tending to innumerable tasks outside their watches. In the morning, the keeper cranked up three 150-pound weights, latched them, and then released them at dusk when the lamp was lit. The weights helped turn the lens. Keepers saved fuel by putting out the light come morning. They closed the lantern room curtains to avert damage and discoloration from amplified sunlight through the lens. Pictured here is the lantern room where the curtains hung to protect the lens.

Keepers carried a five-gallon can, seen here, up to the lantern room with enough fuel to last the 15-to-18-hour period. The quantity depended on the season, as long winter nights needed more oil than summer evenings. They returned with the remaining oil so as not to leave it near an open flame. "Uncovered lights are not to be used in store rooms or closets. When it becomes necessary to enter a store-room or closet with a light, it must be kept in a close lantern," according to the official *Lighthouse Establishment Instructions to Light Keepers*. Keepers kept busy writing reports, requesting supplies, and keeping usage accounts of them. They also trimmed wicks, replaced mantles, pumped up oil vaporizer, and cleaned and lubricated clockwork. The team made specific solutions, fresh each time, to carefully clean and polish the glass prisms, the windows, the glass chimney, and all the metalwork. (Courtesy of the Mariners Museum and Park.)

The regulations covered a lot of ground. Intoxicated persons were not allowed on-site. The grounds, pictured here, and all buildings, inside and out, were kept clean, orderly, and in good repair. This included painting the lighthouse. The men gained a working knowledge of all apparatuses. Rules called for asking questions when in doubt, especially of the visiting lampist and machinist. Understanding the machinery and lens was essential. Specialists did not live on the island and had to travel a good distance to reach the remote Outer Banks. Being able to fix broken machinery went a long way in keeping things in working order.

Keepers signed in and out of evenly divided watch periods. Whoever was on duty had to remain in the watch room keeping his attention on the light. If there was no assistant, the keeper had to visit the light twice between the hours of 8:00 p.m. and sunrise. Leon Wesley Austin served at the Cape Hatteras Lighthouse as a first, second, and third assistant from 1885 to 1893. Austin would have shared the watch with the other keeper(s). During stormy weather, the watch was constant. It was essential to keep an eye out for shipwrecks and administer aid "as was within their power." Reports had to include if the ship in distress had seen or not seen the light. If there were no keepers on-site, a family member would do the watch. The last lightkeeper, Unaka Jennette, pictured here polishing the Cape Hatteras Lighthouse lens, and his wife, Jenny Luanna (known as Sudie), had seven children. Rany Jennette, the fourth child (b. 1921), helped with lighthouse chores, including shining brass. He combined his visits to the top of the lighthouse with fun; using bits of cloth and string, he made parachutes and released them from the towering structure. (Courtesy of the National Geographic Society.)

Keepers and their families lived at the lighthouse site. There could be as many as four keepers employed at the lighthouse along with their wives and children. Rany Jennette recalled their home environment as windy and without dunes. The property included a sedge and big pond, which were home to a number of creatures, including turtles, fish, and ducks. There was also rubble from the first lighthouse located to the south. Some lighthouse keepers and their families led solitary lives, although Cape Hatteras was not isolated. The town of Buxton was a stone's throw away, and the lifesaving station was nearby. Come summertime, local folk living in the woods would seek sea breezes and head to the lighthouse. The children swam, beachcombed, played games, and tooled around in skiffs. Visitors climbed the sentinel. Seen here is a vintage photograph of two children at the lighthouse.

The keepers and their families had vegetable gardens, and livestock roamed freely, as seen here. Vegetation grew on the island, including island species such as wax myrtle and yaupon. Keepers had to carefully care for the lawns. While self-sufficiency was a way of life at the lighthouse site, such as collecting rainwater for drinking and washing, it is important to keep in mind that the lighthouse station was a center of the community. The Cape Hatteras Lighthouse is seen in background.

Seven

A Bright Today and Beyond

The lighthouse was first lit on December 16, 1870. The 150th anniversary was held in 2020. While people enjoy soaking in its memorable past, lighthouse lovers, historians, and its caretakers also look to the future—keeping this remarkable structure shipshape for sailors and visitors to come. Pictured here is the entrance to the historic Cape Hatteras Light Station of today. The visitor center, also seen in this photograph, offers orientation information, off-road vehicle beach permits for purchase, and a park store. The visitor center includes the Cape Hatteras Lighthouse ticket booth, a pavilion for ranger programs, and restroom facilities. (Courtesy of John Havel.)

Shown here is a ring of foundation stones that were left to mark the former site of the Cape Hatteras Lighthouse. In 2001, the names of the 83 keepers who served at the lighthouse were engraved into the granite blocks. Originally marking the place the lighthouse stood before it was moved in 1999, the so-called "Circle of Stones" was covered by sand over the years. (Courtesy of John Havel.)

The picture above shows where the stones were relocated in 2015 by the National Park Service, Outer Banks Lighthouse Society, and Hatteras Island Genealogical and Preservation Society. On November 7, 2015, the National Park Service formally dedicated the Keepers of the Light Amphitheater on the grounds of the Cape Hatteras Light Station in Buxton where the stones were relocated. The stones weighed between 2,300 pounds to 5,700 pounds. (Courtesy of John Havel.)

Just past the Cape Hatteras Lighthouse ticket booth is the Double Keepers' Quarters Museum, formerly the Museum of the Sea, a two-story museum containing exhibits on Outer Banks history, natural history, and the Cape Hatteras Lighthouse relocation. A small audiovisual room provides a video presentation on the relocation of the lighthouse and a tour of inside the lighthouse. The museum is located in what used to be the 1854 Cape Hatteras Lighthouse double keepers' quarters, seen here. (Courtesy of John Havel.)

The structure pictured here is the Cape Hatteras Lighthouse principal keepers' quarters, built in 1871. Today, the building is used for park staff. In 1871, a brick dwelling for the principal keeper was completed from brick left over from building the lighthouse tower. Noted in the front of the picture is a white vinyl fence, not historic, which was put in place in 2000 after the relocation of the lighthouse. Note the shadow of the Cape Hatteras Lighthouse. (Courtesy of John Havel.)

Shown here is the entrance to the Cape Hatteras Lighthouse: a symbolic and very real entrance into a history that continues to fascinate visitors, researchers, photographers, and readers today. (Courtesy of John Havel.)

The historic grounds of the Cape Hatteras Light Station include an admirer, a young local lad named Mason Midgett, taking in the view of the towering structure. The oil house is seen to the left of the lighthouse. In 1892, the annual report of the United States Lighthouse Board called for a brick oil house to be built measuring 15 feet, 6 inches by 13 feet, 6 inches, "with walls 8 feet, 6 inches high and 9 inches thick, and a gable roof 4 feet high." The structure later housed an auxiliary generator for the beacon when the Coast Guard took over operation. Today, the oil house is used by lighthouse staff for storage. The floor is made of brick laid in a herringbone pattern.

Today, visitors can climb the lighthouse and enjoy the incredible views from the top. The climb is strenuous, so be prepared for a workout. Picture here is a National Park Service ranger providing visitors a safety talk before entering the lighthouse. Except under unusual circumstances, the Cape Hatteras Lighthouse is open for self-guided climbs from the third Friday in April through Columbus Day.

Pictured here are visitors entering the lighthouse for a tour. There are 257 steps, the equivalent of walking up the stairs of a 12-story building. It can be hot and humid, so it may not be the right activity for those with some medical conditions. Park rangers greet the excited visitors who come from all over the world to see the iconic structure, one of the most popular sites on the North Carolina Outer Banks.

Pictured here in July 1963 is a district naturalist talking with children inside the Cape Hatteras Lighthouse. Rangers are available on-site to answer questions. Each climber must be at least 42 inches (107 cm) tall and capable of climbing all steps on her or his own. Children 11 years of age or younger must be accompanied by an adult who is 16 years of age or older.

This 2020 photograph shows the view from the balcony of the Cape Hatteras Lighthouse facing north toward Buxton, which is an unincorporated community of nearly 1,500 people located on Hatteras Island, part of the Outer Banks. It is a quiet little village but is well known due to being the home of the Cape Hatteras Lighthouse and one of the nation's finest surf fishing spots, known as "The Point" by local anglers.

This scenic photograph shows, from left to right, John Havel, researcher of the Cape Hatteras Lighthouse; Jami Lanier, cultural resource manager, Cape Hatteras National Seashore; and Doug Stover, retired cultural resource manager, Cape Hatteras National Seashore, with the Atlantic Ocean visible from the balcony of the lighthouse in the background. "Today, the base of the lighthouse lies 1,500 feet from the shore, with a light visible 24 nautical miles out to sea (a nautical mile is 6,080 feet)," according to an article written by John Havel in the Outer Banks Lighthouse Society newsletter *Lighthouse News*. (Courtesy of John Havel.)

According to an article written by John Havel in the Outer Banks Lighthouse Society newsletter *Lighthouse News*, "Seen here is a view from the Cape Hatteras Lighthouse balcony of the double keepers' quarters, built in 1854, and the principal keepers' quarters, built in 1870. The keepers of the Cape Hatteras Lighthouse and their families lived on-site; the keeper had the single structure while the assistant keepers had the larger structures to share." (Courtesy of John Havel.)

The Outer Banks can be a beachcomber's paradise, with miles of shoreline to explore, hidden beaches that are relatively untouched, and piles of shells literally washing up on the beaches after a storm. Shelling on the Outer Banks beaches is simply a matter of timing and area expertise. On one shelling occasion at Cape Point after a storm, there were layers upon layers of shells of a wide variety as far as the eye could see.

Surf fishing at Cape Point within the Cape Hatteras National Seashore offers the angler a variety of excellent fishing opportunities from the Gulf Stream, Atlantic Ocean, and the inlets. At Cape Point, visitors will see waters dramatically crashing together, and they may be lucky enough to catch a red drum. As one can see here, it is not unusual for anglers to be lined up like sentinels along the shore.

The National Park Service off-road vehicle (ORV) management plan permits the use of vehicles on designated ORV routes (ocean and sound-side routes) to help protect the park's treasured resources. This 1950 photograph shows how recreation vehicles have always been part of seashore activities. (Photograph by Aycock Brown.)

The Cape Hatteras National Seashore was established in 1953. According to the *Coastland Times*, more than 451,849 recreational visitors came to the Cape Hatteras National Seashore in July 2020. Pictured here is a view of the much-loved Cape Hatteras Lighthouse.

Considered one of Hatteras Island's biggest attractions, the Cape Hatteras Lighthouse, pictured above, draws over 175,000 visitors every year to climb the 257 steps to the top.

Hurricanes are not the only hazard lapping at the shores of the Outer Banks. There is also the threat of climate change on the natural and cultural landscapes. Due to rising sea levels and erosion, Cape Hatteras National Seashore is disappearing. These photographs show recent impact due to sea-level rise and climate change when a portion of a the 150-year-old brick fence that once surrounded the Cape Hatteras Lighthouse was exposed by ocean waves that carved a cliff into the sand in June 2020. (Both, courtesy of John Havel.)

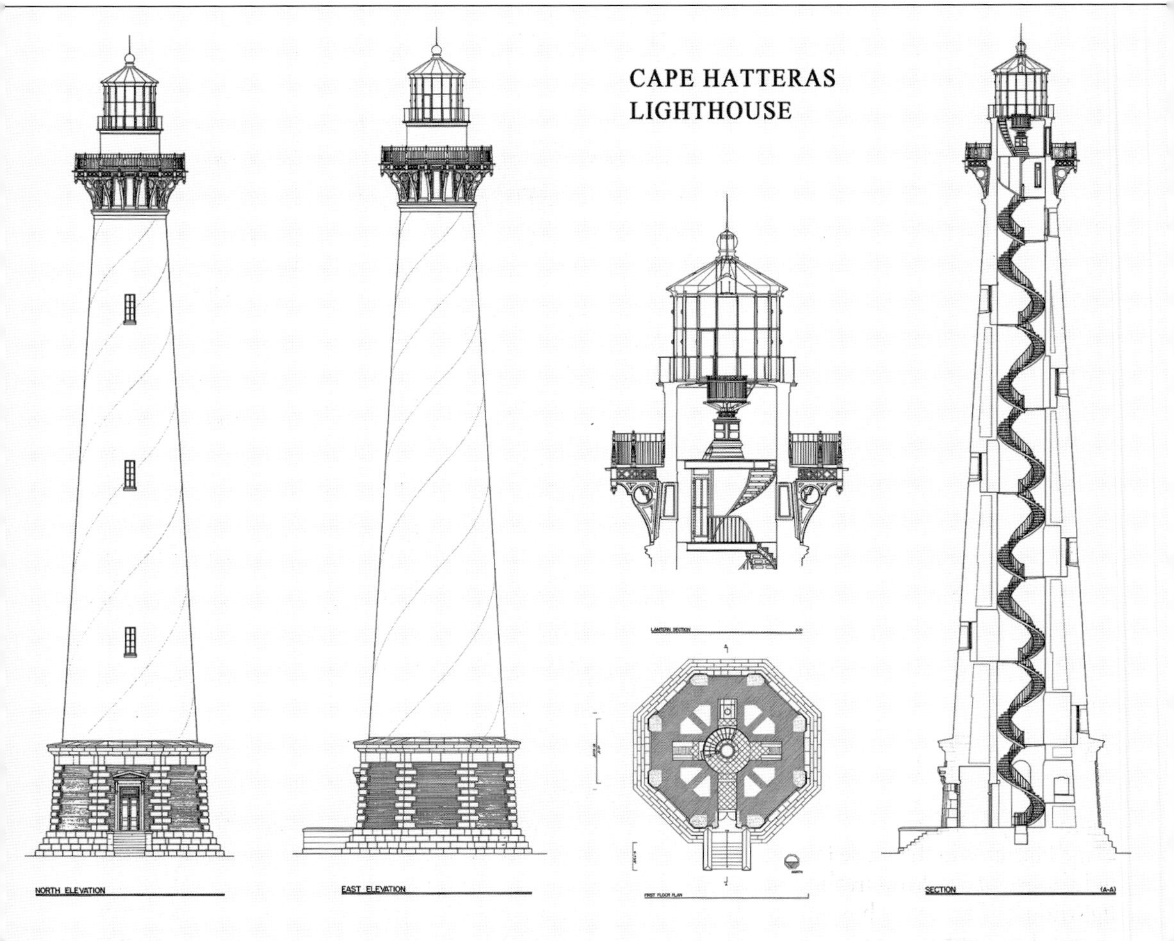

In keeping with carefully tending to the lighthouse and its buildings and grounds, local, state, regional, and national officials, advocates, and supporters are joining forces to prepare for a major restoration project slated to begin in 2021. Shown here is a plan of the Cape Hatteras Lighthouse.

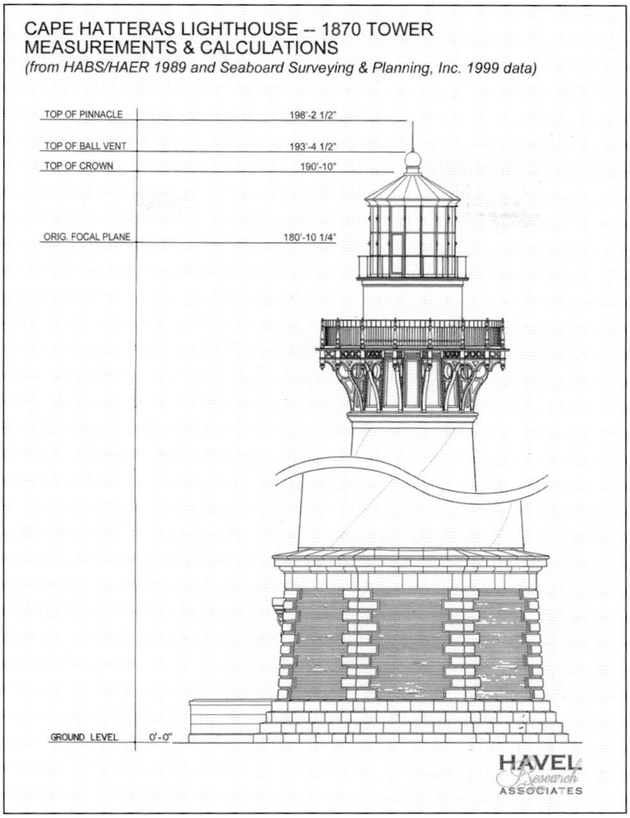

According to information from Rebecca Cybularz's *Cape Hatteras Historic Structure Report*, the Cape Hatteras Lighthouse is the tallest brick lighthouse in the United States as well as the tallest lighthouse of any kind in the state of North Carolina. Here are the specific details regarding the lighthouse. The tower has two heights—193.20 feet (ground to lighthouse peak) and 198.49 feet (ground to lightning rod). The focal height (mean sea level to light) is 192.2 feet. The column height is 147 feet, 4.5 inches, and the diameter is 32 feet, 5.5 inches. The height above mean sea level at the old site was 208.0 feet, and the height above mean sea level at the new site is 210.01 feet. The lower gallery height above the sidewalk is 165 feet, .5 inches. The weight of the lighthouse, not including the foundation, is 4,830 tons. The lighthouse exterior uses between 140 and 150 gallons of paint. There are two black stripes, and the stripe rotations around the column are 1.5. Various details on the windows includes the following: height is 6 feet, 5 inches; width is 2 feet, 4.5 inches; and the window pattern is staggered. There are seven windows, three on the entrance side and four on the opposite side, and the spacing between same-side windows is 40 feet, .5 inches. The base structure is octagonal in shape with a bottom diameter of 37 feet, 5 inches; a top diameter of 32 feet, 6 inches; and a height of 21 feet, 9.5 inches. There are two doors on the lighthouse both with a height of 10 feet, 5.5 inches; a width of 4 feet, 4 inches; a doorway width of 8 feet, 8 inches; and a frame width of 1 foot, 4 inches. The stairs in this lighthouse are a story all their own. From the sidewalk to the lantern room, there are 269 steps; visitors may only climb 257 of those (the height of a visitors' climb reaches a little more that 166 feet). There are nine granite steps at the base with a rise of eight inches. Interestingly, the depth of the steps changes: The first seven have a depth of 11 inches; the eighth has a depth of 2 feet, 9 inches; and the ninth has a 3-foot depth. There are 248 cast-iron steps to the floor of the watch room with a width of 33 inches and rise of 7 feet, .75 inches—seven flights with 31 steps each (with a weight of 5,000 pounds for each flight), one flight with 16, and another with 15. There are then 12 companionway steps to the upper gallery in the lantern area.

The National Park Service's Denver Service Center's Design and Construction Division, which was involved in the restoration of the Washington Monument, will be overseeing the lighthouse's major restoration project, slated to begin in the summer of 2021. To carry out this major renovation, designers, engineers, planners, and other invested parties gathered to review the restoration goals. The project will include repairs, replacement, or restoration to deteriorated masonry, metal components, windows, and marble flooring. The restoration project will restore many of the rusted cast-iron features of the historic lighthouse, including windows, doors, the balcony, and other architectural elements. Pictured here is the Cape Hatteras Lighthouse tower. (Courtesy of John Havel.)

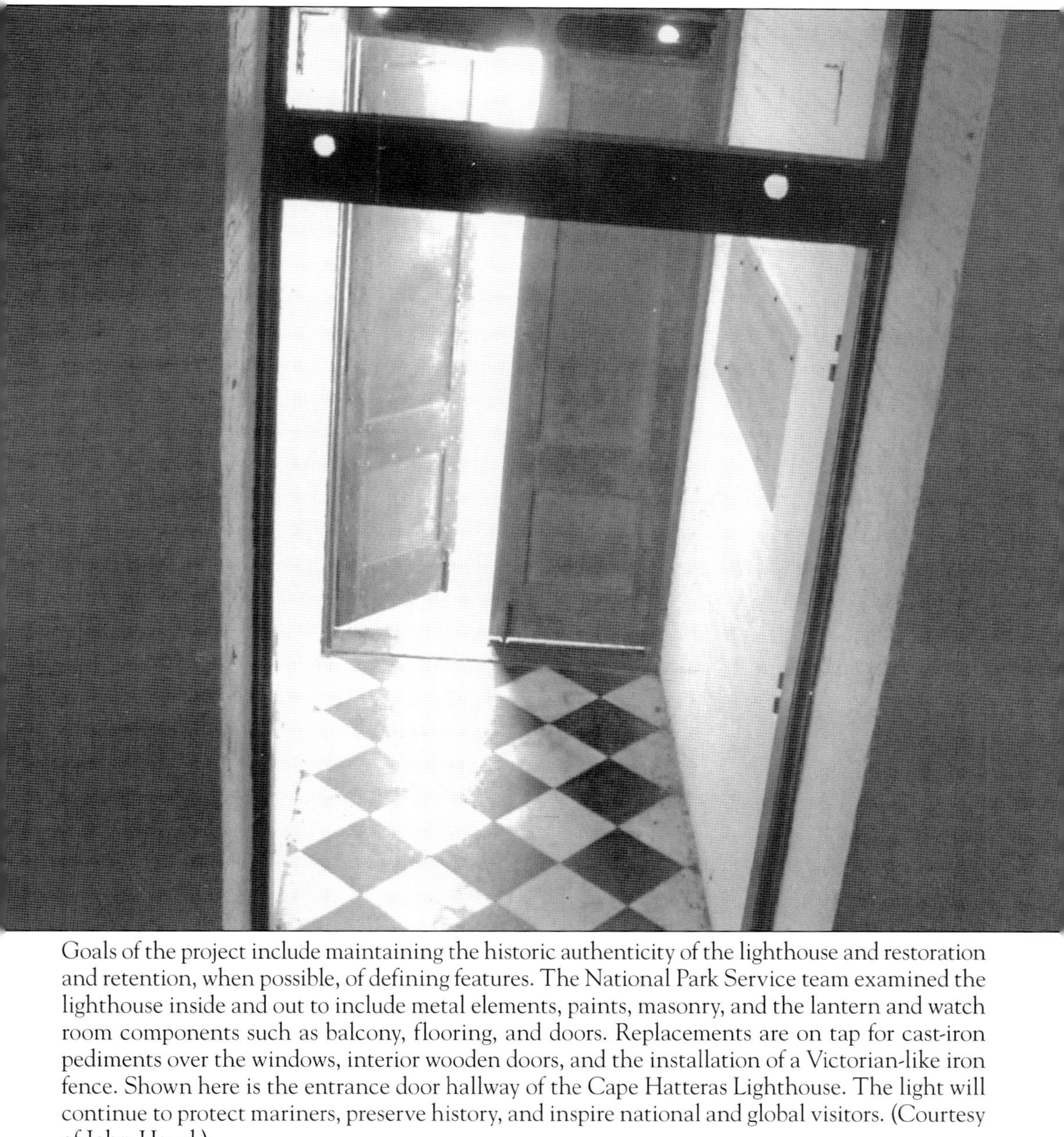

Goals of the project include maintaining the historic authenticity of the lighthouse and restoration and retention, when possible, of defining features. The National Park Service team examined the lighthouse inside and out to include metal elements, paints, masonry, and the lantern and watch room components such as balcony, flooring, and doors. Replacements are on tap for cast-iron pediments over the windows, interior wooden doors, and the installation of a Victorian-like iron fence. Shown here is the entrance door hallway of the Cape Hatteras Lighthouse. The light will continue to protect mariners, preserve history, and inspire national and global visitors. (Courtesy of John Havel.)

According to an article written by John Havel in the Outer Banks Lighthouse Society newsletter *Lighthouse News*, "The restoration/retention of the Cape Hatteras Lighthouse is an ongoing, massive project with lots of details. As the history of the lighthouse shows, the work can uncover elements to address as the project moves forward. The initial plans are being made to begin a major repair project that will give the Cape Hatteras Lighthouse a well-deserved restoration from the inside out. Seen here are tile floors, of which about 100 will need to be replaced due to cracks. The plastic netting and steel mesh floor were put down by the National Park Service for safety purposes. This was originally a sand pit that was provided in case the weight cable of the clockwork mechanism parted causing the weight to free-fall down the tower. The sand pit was much more forgiving and flexible than the slate and marble floor that surrounds the pit. The weight set could also be lowered into the pit to facilitate maintenance and repairs such as cable repair or replacement. The well is about four feet deep." (Courtesy of John Havel.)

"The Cape Hatteras Lighthouse repair project will include repairs to deteriorated masonry, metal components, windows, and marble flooring. It will also restore important architectural components, including missing pediments over the lighthouse windows and missing interior doors, according to the 2014 Comprehensive Condition Assessment Report and a 2016 Historic Structure Report. Shown here is the large, square, 350-gallon tank that was used for the storage of kerosene to light the lamp in the Fresnel lens," according to an article written by John Havel in the Outer Banks Lighthouse Society newsletter *Lighthouse News*. (Courtesy of John Havel.)

This photograph shows weights of the lens clockwork suspended wire cable through the center of the interior of the lighthouse with a T-rail to keep the weights from swinging into the stairs, according to the *Cape Hatteras Lighthouse Historic Structure Report* by historic architect Rebecca Cybularz, National Park Service, in February 2016. (Courtesy of John Havel.)

According to an article written by John Havel in the Outer Banks Lighthouse Society newsletter *Lighthouse News*, "The restoration effort will focus on historic fabric that can be saved, meaning any original material or part of the building, as the lighthouse is a national historic landmark, and historic fabric must be saved, if possible, or repaired. Seen here is a window on the Cape Hatteras Lighthouse; the metal windows that are deteriorating or rusting need work, and some of the brick and mortar components also need refurbishing. Some of the windows in the current lighthouse have been replaced, but a few are original." (Courtesy of John Havel.)

"There is a long list of items that will need to be addressed, including repairs to deteriorated masonry, metal components, windows, and marble flooring. The list also includes replacing missing interior doors and repairing doors as needed, as well as replacing doorknobs and hinges. Rotted wood and rusted metal will be dealt with as well," according to an article written by John Havel in the Outer Banks Lighthouse Society newsletter *Lighthouse News*. (Courtesy of John Havel.)

Pictured at right is the staircase to the lens room, which is off limits to visitors. Today's beacon is seen below. The aerobeacon flashes every 7.5 seconds. Though the lighthouse itself is owned and managed by the National Park Service, the US Coast Guard operates and maintains the automated light. (Both, courtesy of John Havel.)

US Coast Guard electrician's mate first class James Harper and US Coast Guard aids to navigation team member Ben Atherholt are pictured here. The men replaced the motor that rotates the beam. (Courtesy of John Havel.)

The photograph here shows one of the men continuing the motor replacement project. The beacon at the top of the Cape Hatteras Lighthouse had stopped rotating after a powerful nor'easter impacted the Outer Banks in 2020. (Courtesy of John Havel.)

The future of replacing the beacon with a reproduction of a first-order Fresnel lens has been discussed as an option for a future beacon, but budget costs and US Coast Guard navigation standards would have to be met. Today, reproduction lens prisms are available in acrylic or glass. The acrylic prisms can be matched to the original green color as well as the size and thickness of the historic lens. Pictured here is Doug Stover, retired historian for Cape Hatteras National Seashore.

Scaffolding is visible around the top of the balcony. A 200-foot crane was used to put up the scaffolding; people used it to replace ironwork in 1991. In the 2021 restoration and rehabilitation, damaged cast-iron metal will be replaced with metal less prone to rusting.

These two photographs show ironwork that needs to be addressed in the rehabilitation and repair process. This includes making sure a list of things are shipshape: the cast-iron brackets that brace the support of the lantern room, the stair steps and supports, railing, and the gallery deck railing and balcony rail post. The lighthouse will be thoroughly examined to address all balcony issues to ensure the safety of visitors standing there.

Visitors and lighthouse fans can look forward to a face-lift and a fresh paint job. The National Park Service paints the Cape Hatteras Lighthouse every seven years to keep it looking pristine and historically authentic, utilizing roughly 450 gallons of paint for multiple coats. Contracted workers suspend from the balcony and paint down the lighthouse alternating between black and white paint along the stripe. In the photograph above, workers clean the lighthouse before painting it. The paint is a vital piece of the lighthouse's iconic look.

Here, workers are painting the historic black-and-white lighthouse. The stripes serve as a daytime identification aid—known as a daymark—allowing mariners to distinguish between the lighthouses. Workers will also be installing the 1870 Victorian cast-iron fence around the lighthouse, replacing the vinyl, two-rail fence that was put in place after the move of the Cape Hatteras Lighthouse in 1999. The lighthouse was originally painted red on top and white on the bottom. In 1873, it was painted with white-and-black striped daymarks.

Cape Hatteras National Seashore celebrated the 20th anniversary of the Cape Hatteras Lighthouse move on July 1, 2019. National Parks of Eastern North Carolina superintendent David Hallac, seen here, greeted the public at the special event celebrating the anniversary of the epic move that saved the iconic structure. (Courtesy of John Havel.)